THE COMPLETE DIABETIC AIR FRYER COOKBOOK

1500 Days Of Air Fryer Adventures For Diabetes Management| Full Color Pictures Version

NADIA K. THEISEN

EDITOR: LYN

COVER ART: ABR

INTERIOR DESIGN: FAIZAN

FOOD STYLIST: JO

Table of Contents

Introduction

In today's health-conscious world, finding innovative ways to enjoy delicious meals while maintaining a balanced diet is a top priority. Enter the air fryer, a kitchen appliance that has taken the culinary world by storm. with its promise of crispy and flavorful dishes using minimal oil, the air fryer has revolutionized the way we approach healthy cooking. From guilt-free French fries to succulent chicken wings, the air fryer offers a tantalizing alternative to traditional deep frying methods. Join us as we explore the wonders of this remarkable appliance and discover how it can transform your culinary experience while promoting a healthier lifestyle.

Air fryers can be a valuable addition to the kitchen for individuals who suffer from diabetes. with their innovative cooking method, air fryers offer several advantages that can support a diabetes-friendly diet and help manage blood sugar levels effectively.

One of the primary benefits of air fryers is their ability to cook food using hot air circulation, requiring little to no oil. This feature significantly reduces the fat content of meals, which is crucial for individuals with diabetes. By minimizing the consumption of unhealthy fats, such as saturated and trans fats, air fryers assist in maintaining a heart-healthy diet. This is particularly important as people with diabetes are at a higher risk of cardiovascular complications.

In addition to reducing the fat content, air fryers also promote lower calorie intake. By using significantly less oil compared to traditional frying methods, air fryers help decrease the calorie content of fried foods. This can be beneficial for individuals with diabetes who need to manage their weight or reduce calorie intake to control blood sugar levels. By making healthier versions of favorite fried foods, such as crispy vegetables or air-fried chicken, individuals can enjoy the flavors and textures they love without compromising their health.

Another advantage of air fryers is their versatility. They can be used for more than just frying. Air fryers can bake, roast, grill, and even reheat food. This versatility encourages the inclusion of a wide range of nutritious foods in the diet, such as lean meats, fish, and vegetables. By using an air fryer to cook these foods without excessive oil or breading, individuals can reduce their carbohydrate and calorie intake while still enjoying delicious and satisfying meals.

It is important to note that while air fryers offer health benefits for individuals with diabetes, it is still essential to focus on the overall quality and balance of the diet. Incorporating a variety of nutrient-dense foods, monitoring portion sizes, and considering individual dietary needs are key factors in managing diabetes effectively.

In conclusion, air fryers can be a valuable tool for individuals with diabetes. Their ability to cook food with minimal oil, reduce fat and calorie content, and promote the inclusion of nutritious foods make them a convenient and beneficial appliance for diabetes management.

Chapter 1
Understanding Diabetes and Healthy Eating

Diabetes and Obesity

Diabetes and obesity are two interconnected health conditions that pose significant challenges to individuals and society as a whole. Both conditions have reached epidemic proportions globally and can have severe consequences for one's health and well-being. Understanding the relationship between diabetes and obesity is crucial in order to effectively address and manage these conditions.

Obesity, characterized by excessive body weight and high levels of body fat, increases the risk of developing type 2 diabetes. The accumulation of visceral fat, particularly around the abdomen, leads to insulin resistance—a condition in which the body's cells become less responsive to the hormone insulin. This impaired insulin function results in elevated blood sugar levels, eventually leading to the development of diabetes.

On the other hand, diabetes itself can contribute to weight gain and the progression of obesity. The inability of the body to properly regulate blood sugar levels in diabetes can lead to increased hunger and cravings, as well as a reduced ability to burn stored fat for energy. Additionally, certain diabetes medications may promote weight gain as a side effect, further exacerbating the obesity-diabetes cycle.

Diabetes Types

Diabetes is a chronic medical condition characterized by high levels of blood glucose, commonly referred to as blood sugar. There are several types of diabetes, each with its own unique characteristics. Let's explore the details of each type:

TYPE 1 DIABETES

Type 1 diabetes, also known as insulin-dependent diabetes or juvenile-onset diabetes, is an autoimmune disease. It occurs when the immune system mistakenly attacks and destroys the insulin-producing cells in the pancreas. As a result, the body produces little to no insulin. Individuals with type 1 diabetes require lifelong insulin therapy to regulate blood sugar levels. This type of diabetes is typically diagnosed in children, adolescents, or young adults, although it can occur at any age.

TYPE 2 DIABETES

Type 2 diabetes, also known as non-insulin-dependent diabetes or adult-onset diabetes, is the most common type of diabetes. It occurs when the body becomes resistant to the effects of insulin or when the pancreas fails to produce enough insulin to meet the body's needs. Type 2 diabetes is often associated with lifestyle factors such as poor diet, sedentary behavior, obesity, and genetic predisposition. Initially, it can often be managed with lifestyle modifications including diet, exercise, and weight loss. However, as the condition progresses, medication or insulin therapy may be necessary.

GESTATIONAL DIABETES

Gestational diabetes develops during pregnancy and usually resolves after childbirth. It occurs when the hormones produced during pregnancy interfere with insulin action, leading to high blood sugar levels. Gestational diabetes requires careful monitoring and management to prevent complications for both the mother and the baby. Women who have had gestational diabetes are at increased risk of developing type 2 diabetes later in life.

OTHER TYPES OF DIABETES

There are also other less common types of diabetes, including:

LADA (Latent Autoimmune Diabetes in Adults): This form of diabetes shares characteristics of both type 1 and type 2 diabetes and is often misdiagnosed as type 2 diabetes initially.

MODY (Maturity-Onset Diabetes of the Young): This is a rare genetic form of diabetes that typically develops before the age of 25 and is caused by specific gene mutations.

Secondary Diabetes: This type of diabetes is caused by certain medical conditions, medications, or hormonal disorders.

Healthy Habits of Living and Eating

BALANCED AND NUTRITIOUS DIET

A balanced diet is essential for individuals with diabetes. It should include a variety of nutrient-dense foods. Focus on incorporating:

- Fruits and vegetables: These provide essential vitamins, minerals, and fiber. Aim for a colorful variety to maximize nutrient intake.
- Lean proteins: Include sources such as skinless chicken, fish, tofu, legumes, and low-fat dairy products. Proteins help maintain muscle mass and contribute to overall satiety.
- Whole grains: Opt for whole grain bread, brown rice, quinoa, and oats, which provide more fiber and nutrients compared to refined grains.
- Healthy fats: Incorporate sources like avocados, nuts, seeds, and olive oil. These provide essential fatty acids and help promote heart health.

REGULAR MEAL TIMES

Consistency in meal timing is crucial for managing blood sugar levels. Aim to have meals at consistent intervals throughout the day, such as breakfast, lunch, and dinner, with healthy snacks in between if needed. This helps regulate glucose levels and supports optimal diabetes management.

CARBOHYDRATE COUNTING

Carbohydrates have the most significant impact on blood sugar levels. Learning to count carbohydrates and incorporating them into meal planning can help individuals with diabetes manage their glucose levels effectively. Consult with a registered dietitian or diabetes educator to learn about carbohydrate counting and how to match insulin doses or adjust medication accordingly.

GLYCEMIC CONTROL

Maintaining stable blood sugar levels is a key aspect of diabetes management. Alongside carbohydrate counting, monitoring portion sizes and adjusting medication as advised by healthcare professionals can help achieve optimal glycemic control. Regular blood sugar monitoring using a glucometer or continuous glucose monitoring system can provide insights into patterns and trends, enabling better management.

FIBER-RICH FOODS

High-fiber foods are beneficial for individuals with diabetes. They promote slower digestion, preventing rapid spikes in blood sugar levels. Include sources of dietary fiber such as whole grains, legumes, fruits, and vegetables in your meals. Gradually increase fiber intake to avoid digestive discomfort, and drink plenty of water to aid digestion.

HEALTHY FATS

Healthy fats play a role in heart health and overall well-being. Include sources such as avocados, nuts, seeds, and olive oil in your diet. These fats provide essential fatty acids and can contribute to satiety. However, remember that fats are high in calories, so portion control is important.

REGULAR PHYSICAL ACTIVITY

Regular exercise is vital for individuals with diabetes. Engaging in physical activity helps improve insulin sensitivity, promotes weight management, and enhances overall cardiovascular health. Aim for at least 150 minutes of moderate-intensity aerobic activity (such as brisk walking) per week, along with strength training exercises twice a week.

PORTION CONTROL

Practicing portion control helps manage calorie intake and blood sugar levels. Use smaller plates and bowls to visually trick your mind into feeling satisfied with smaller portions. Measure portions when cooking or use visual cues to estimate appropriate serving sizes. Being mindful of portion sizes can prevent overeating and support weight management.

HYDRATION

Staying hydrated is important for overall health, including managing blood sugar levels. Drink plenty of water throughout the day. Avoid sugary beverages, as they can cause spikes in blood sugar. Aim for at least 8 cups (64 ounces) of water daily, but individual needs may vary based on factors such as activity level and climate.

STRESS MANAGEMENT

Stress can affect blood sugar levels. Finding healthy ways to manage stress is essential for individuals with diabetes. Engage in activities such as meditation, deep breathing exercises, yoga, or hobbies that help you relax and unwind. Regular exercise, spending time with loved ones, and seeking support from a therapist or support group can also be beneficial.

REGULAR MONITORING

Monitoring blood sugar levels regularly is crucial for managing diabetes effectively. It provides valuable information about how certain foods, activities, medications, and stress levels affect your glucose levels. Regular monitoring empowers you to make informed decisions about your diet and lifestyle choices.

REGULAR CHECK-UPS

Regular check-ups with your healthcare team, including your doctor, registered dietitian, and diabetes educator, are essential. These professionals can assess your overall health, review your diabetes management plan, address any concerns, and provide guidance and support tailored to your specific needs. Regular check-ups help ensure that you stay on track with your diabetes management goals and make any necessary adjustments to your plan.

Features and Benefits of Air Fryers

Air fryers have gained popularity as a cooking appliance due to their unique features and benefits. When it comes to diabetes management, air fryers can be a valuable tool. Let's explore the features and benefits of air fryers, especially in relation to diabetes:

HEALTHIER COOKING METHOD

Air fryers use hot air circulation and a minimal amount of oil to cook food, resulting in a crispy texture similar to deep-frying but with significantly less oil. This can be beneficial for individuals with diabetes who need to manage their fat intake and reduce the consumption of fried foods.

REDUCED OIL USAGE

Air fryers require only a fraction of the oil typically used in traditional deep-frying methods. By using significantly less oil, individuals with diabetes can reduce their calorie and fat intake, which may contribute to better blood sugar control and weight management.

LOWER GLYCEMIC IMPACT

Air frying allows for the preparation of a wide variety of foods, including vegetables, lean meats, and whole grains. These types of foods tend to have a lower glycemic index (GI) compared to heavily processed and fried foods. Lower-GI foods help regulate blood sugar levels, making air-fried meals a diabetes-friendly option.

VERSATILE COOKING OPTIONS

Air fryers offer versatility in cooking. They can bake, grill, roast, and even reheat leftovers. This versatility allows individuals with diabetes to prepare a variety of healthy meals and snacks using different cooking methods, resulting in a more balanced and enjoyable diet.

TIME AND ENERGY EFFICIENCY

Air fryers typically cook food faster than traditional oven baking. They also require less preheating time, which can be beneficial for busy individuals. Additionally, air fryers are more energy-efficient than conventional ovens, helping to reduce overall energy consumption.

EASY CLEANUP

Air fryers are designed to be user-friendly and often come with removable, non-stick cooking baskets or trays that are easy to clean. This makes meal preparation and cleanup hassle-free, allowing individuals with diabetes to focus on their overall health and well-being.

PORTION CONTROL

Air fryers generally have smaller cooking capacities, which can promote portion control. By cooking smaller quantities at a time, individuals with diabetes can better manage portion sizes and avoid overeating.

RETENTION OF NUTRIENTS

Air frying retains more nutrients compared to deep-frying, as there is minimal exposure to excessive heat and oil. This can be advantageous for individuals with diabetes, as they can enjoy meals that retain more of the essential vitamins, minerals, and fiber present in the ingredients.

When using an air fryer, it's important to choose diabetes-friendly recipes and ingredients. Opt for lean proteins, whole grains, and plenty of vegetables. Minimize the use of added sugars, saturated fats, and processed ingredients. It's also crucial to monitor portion sizes and overall calorie intake to support blood sugar management.

Mastering Air Fryer Techniques

Mastering air fryer techniques involves familiarizing yourself with the appliance and understanding how to optimize its use. Here are some tips to help you become proficient in air fryer cooking:

Read the Manual
Start by thoroughly reading the user manual that comes with your air fryer. This will provide important information about its specific features, functions, and safety guidelines.

Preheat the Air Fryer
Preheating the air fryer before cooking is essential for optimal results. Follow the manufacturer's instructions for preheating time and temperature, as this ensures that the food cooks evenly and achieves the desired crispness.

UNDERSTAND COOKING TEMPERATURES

Different foods require different cooking temperatures in an air fryer. Familiarize yourself with the recommended cooking temperatures for various ingredients, such as meats, vegetables, and baked goods. This knowledge will help you achieve the desired results.

ADJUST COOKING TIME

Air fryers cook food faster than traditional methods, so it's important to adjust the cooking time accordingly. Start by following recipes or guidelines, but be prepared to make adjustments based on the specific model of your air fryer and the desired level of doneness.

USE THE RIGHT AMOUNT OF OIL

While air fryers require less oil than traditional frying methods, a small amount of oil can enhance the flavor and texture of your dishes. Use a cooking spray or lightly brush the food with oil to achieve a crispy and golden exterior.

ARRANGE FOOD IN A SINGLE LAYER

To ensure even cooking, arrange the food in a single layer in the air fryer basket. Avoid overcrowding, as this can prevent proper air circulation and result in unevenly cooked food.

SHAKE OR FLIP THE FOOD

During the cooking process, periodically shake or flip the food to promote even browning. This is especially important for foods like French fries, chicken wings, or vegetables to ensure uniform crispness.

EXPERIMENT WITH SEASONINGS AND MARINADES

Air fryers provide a great opportunity to experiment with different seasonings, herbs, and marinades to enhance the flavor of your dishes. Be creative and try out different combinations to find what you enjoy the most.

USE ACCESSORIES

Many air fryers come with additional accessories such as baking pans, grill racks, or skewers. Take advantage of these accessories to expand your cooking options and achieve different textures and flavors.

KEEP THE AIR FRYER CLEAN

Regularly clean your air fryer to prevent the buildup of oil and residue. Refer to the user manual for specific cleaning instructions. A clean air fryer ensures optimal performance and extends the lifespan of the appliance.

Avoiding Common Air Frying Mistakes

OVERCROWDING THE AIR FRYER

One of the most common mistakes is overcrowding the air fryer basket or tray. It's important to leave enough space between the food items to allow proper air circulation. Overcrowding can lead to uneven cooking and less crispy results. Cook in multiple batches if necessary to maintain optimal air flow.

NEGLECTING TO PREHEAT

Preheating the air fryer is crucial for achieving consistent and even cooking. It allows the cooking chamber to reach the desired temperature before adding the food. Skipping the preheating step can result in undercooked or unevenly cooked food. Follow the manufacturer's instructions for preheating time and temperature.

NOT USING OIL OR USING TOO MUCH

While air fryers require less oil than traditional frying methods, some recipes may still call for a small amount of oil. It helps to enhance the flavor and promote browning. However, using too much oil can lead to greasy results. Follow the recipe guidelines or use a light mist of oil to prevent excessive oiliness.

IGNORING FOOD PREPARATION

Properly preparing the food before air frying is crucial. For example, if you're cooking vegetables, ensure they are cut into uniform sizes to ensure even cooking. For meats, pat them dry to remove excess moisture, which can prevent proper browning. Taking the time to prepare the ingredients appropriately will contribute to better results.

NOT SHAKING OR FLIPPING THE FOOD

To promote even browning and prevent sticking, it's important to shake or flip the food during the cooking process. This helps to ensure that all sides are cooked evenly. Set a timer to remind yourself to shake or flip the food at regular intervals, depending on the recipe.

USING INCORRECT TEMPERATURE AND TIME SETTINGS

Every air fryer model is different, so it's important to understand the temperature and time settings specific to your appliance. Follow the recipe guidelines as a starting point but be prepared to make adjustments based on your air fryer's performance and your desired level of doneness.

NEGLECTING TO CHECK FOR DONENESS

It's crucial to check the doneness of the food before assuming it's fully cooked. Use a food thermometer to check the internal temperature of meats or a fork to ensure vegetables are tender. This prevents undercooked or overcooked food and helps you achieve the desired texture and taste.

NOT CLEANING THE AIR FRYER PROPERLY

Regularly cleaning your air fryer is important for maintaining its performance and longevity. Neglecting to clean the removable parts, such as the basket or tray, can result in a buildup of residue and affect the quality of subsequent meals. Refer to the user manual for specific cleaning instructions and ensure the appliance is completely dry before using it again.

In conclusion, mastering the techniques of air frying can be a game-changer, especially for individuals with diabetes. By understanding the features and benefits of air fryers, avoiding common mistakes, and experimenting with recipes, you can harness the full potential of this cooking method. Air frying offers a healthier alternative to traditional frying, with reduced oil usage and lower glycemic impact. It empowers you to enjoy crispy and flavorful meals while managing your blood sugar levels effectively. with practice and a willingness to explore new flavors and techniques, you can become a proficient air fryer chef, creating delicious and diabetes-friendly dishes that contribute to your overall well-being. So, embrace the possibilities of air frying and embark on a culinary journey that combines health and taste.

Chapter 3
Breakfast

Egg in a Hole
Prep time: 5 minutes | Cook time: 8 minutes | Serves 1

- 2 eggs
- salt
- pepper
- 1 tablespoon butter
- bread (2 slices)

1. First, preheat your air fryer to 325° F for 3 minutes.
2. Place a parchment paper round in the basket and butter on both sides of the bread.
3. Use a glass, or you can use a cookie cutter to cut a hole in the center of the bread.
4. Crack an egg into the hole, season with salt and pepper, then cook at 325° F for 6 minutes.
5. Remove from the air fryer and serve.

PER SERVING

Calories: 108 | Fat: 6.2g | Carbs: 5.6g | Protein: 6g

Breakfast Cod Nuggets
Prep time: 10 minutes | Cook time: 10 minutes | Serves 4

- 1 lb. cod
- For Breading:
- 2 eggs, beaten
- 2 tbsp. olive oil
- 1 cup almond flour
- ¾ cup breadcrumbs
- 1 tsp. dried parsley
- Pinch sea salt
- ½ tsp. black pepper

1. Preheat the air fryer to 390°F.
2. Cut the cod into strips about 1-inch by 2-inches. Blend breadcrumbs, olive oil, salt, parsley, and pepper in a food processor.
3. In 3 separate bowls, add breadcrumbs, eggs, and flour. Place each piece of fish into flour, then the eggs, and the breadcrumbs. Add pieces of cod to the air fryer basket and cook for 10 minutes. Serve warm.

PER SERVING

Calories: 212.5 | Fat: 12.2g | Carbs: 8.8g | Protein: 13.6g

Chocolate & Zucchini Muffins
Prep time: 5 minutes | Cook time:36 minutes |Serves 1

- 1 tbsp ground flaxseed
- 3 tbsp water
- ½ cup all-purpose flour
- ¼ cup whole wheat pastry flour
- ¼ cup unsweetened cocoa powder
- ¼ tsp baking soda
- ¼ tsp kosher salt
- ¼ tsp ground cinnamon
- ½ cup granulated sugar

- ¼ cup canola oil
- ½ tsp pure vanilla extract
- ½ tsp freshly squeezed lemon juice
- ¾ cup grated zucchini
- ½ cup vegan chocolate chips

1. Set the air fryer temp to 270°F. Spray 12 silicone muffin cups with nonstick cooking spray. Set aside.
2. In a small bowl, combine the flaxseed and water.
3. In a large bowl, whisk together the all-purpose flour, whole wheat pastry flour, cocoa powder, baking soda, salt, and cinnamon. Add the sugar, canola oil, vanilla extract, lemon juice, and flaxseed mixture. Mix well. Fold in the zucchini and chocolate chips. Place the batter into the muffin cups.
4. Working in batches, place 6 muffin cups in the fryer basket and bake until a toothpick comes out clean from the center of a muffin, about 15 to 18 minutes.
5. Remove the cups from the fryer basket and allow the muffins to cool for 10 minutes before serving.

PER SERVING

Calories: 154 | Fat: 8g | Sat Fat: 1g | Cholesterol:0mg | Sodium: 29mg | Carbohydrates 22g | Fiber:2g | Sugar:8g | Protein:2g

Hash Browns
Prep time: 5 minutes | Cook time: 8 minutes | Serves 4

- 4 potatoes (medium sized)
- ¼ tablespoon freshly ground black pepper
- 1 tablespoon oil
- ½ teaspoon salt

1. To make hash browns, shred the potatoes in a food processor. Put them into a colander and place them under cold water for 1 minute. Drain the colander for a few minutes.
2. Transfer the shredded potatoes to a clean paper towel and press them dry. Make sure to dry them out completely for the crispiest hash browns.
3. Add oil and seasonings to the bowl; mix well before adding to the basket of air fryer set at 380°F for 15 minutes. Flip the basket over and repeat on the other side until desired crispness is reached (it should take another 5-10 minutes).

PER SERVING

Calories: 195kcal | Fat: 4g | Carbs: 37g | Protein: 4g | Sugar: 2g | Sodium: 304mg

Garlic Green Beans with Lemon

Prep time: 5 minutes | Cook time: 8 minutes | Serves 4

- 1 pound green beans
- ½ teaspoon salt
- 1 teaspoon garlic powder
- grated parmesan cheese
- lemon wedges to serve
- 1 tablespoon lemon juice
- ½ teaspoon ground black pepper
- 1 tablespoon olive oi

1. To wash and dry green beans, put them in a colander and rinse under warm water.
2. Trim the ends, spray with olive oil, season with salt, black pepper, and garlic powder (or other spices), then toss to coat.
3. Add lemon juice while they're still wet; they need to be firm enough to hold their shape when cooked.
4. Preheat the Air fryer and set the temperature to 400°F; place the green beans in a basket, and cook for 6-8 minutes without shaking.
5. Transfer from your Air fryer, plate up with melted parmesan cheese and lemon wedges for presentation if you like.

PER SERVING

Calories: 68Kcal | Fat: 4g | Carbs: 8g | Protein: 2g | Sugar: 4g | Sodium: 298mg

Air Fryer Bacon

Prep time: 2 minutes | Cook time: 10 minutes | Serves 5

- 5 slices (thick-cut) bacon

1. Lay the bacon slices into your air fryer basket, at least 1 inch apart, to cook. Heat the air fryer at 390°F. Cook bacon for 10 minutes until crispy.
2. Drain on a kitchen napkin before serving.

PER SERVING

Calories: 102.7 | Fat: 2.5g | Carbs: 0.4g | Fiber: 0g, Sugar: 0g | Protein: 8.3g

Crispy Fried Green Beans

Prep time: 10 minutes | Cook time: 10 minutes | Serves 4

- 1 pound fresh green beans
- 3-4 large eggs
- 1 teaspoon salt
- 1 cup all-purpose flour
- 2 cups Italian seasoned bread crumbs
- 1 teaspoon pepper

1. To make air-fried green beans, wash and trim the beans, then let them dry completely.
2. Spread them out on a large baking sheet and spray with a light layer of cooking spray.
3. In a bowl, combine flour, eggs, seasoned bread crumbs, and salt & pepper.
4. Dip each bean into the flour to coat, then into the beaten eggs, and finally into the seasoned bread crumbs.
5. Working in batches, place beans in your air fryer basket so they are in a single layer.
6. Air fry at 375° F for 5-7 minutes or until golden brown and crispy.
7. Remove from the basket and serve them hot.

PER SERVING

Calories: 226Kcal | Fat: 4g | Carbs: 37g | Protein: 10g | Sugar: 4g | Sodium: 704mg

Black Bean Burger Burritos

Prep time: 20 minutes | Cook time:10 minutes |Serves 1

- 4 black bean burgers
- sriracha chili sauce
- 4 large flour tortillas
- baby spinach
- 1 avocado, diced

1. Set the air fryer temp to 380°F.
2. Place the black bean burgers in the fryer basket and cook for 4 minutes per side.
3. Remove the burgers from the fryer basket and roughly chop. Spread the chili sauce on the tortillas and top with equal amounts of spinach, avocado, and burger. Wrap the tortillas around the filling.
4. Place the burritos in the fryer basket and cook until the tortillas are toasted, about 2 minutes.
5. Remove the burritos from the fryer basket and cut in half. Serve immediately or wrap them in aluminum foil for an on-the-go meal.

PER SERVING

Calories: 357 | Fat: 16g | Sat Fat: 3g | Cholesterol:0mg | Sodium: 770mg | Carbohydrates 42g | Fiber:8g | Sugar:2g | Protein:16g

Crescent Pockets

Prep time: 10 minutes | Cook time: 5 minutes | Serves 8

- 8 ounces packages of refrigerated crescent rolls
- salt and freshly ground black pepper to taste
- 4 large eggs
- 8 ounces maple apple chicken sausage
- 1 tablespoon olive oil

2. Preheat the air fryer to 370 degrees F.
3. Divide the crescent dough into triangles. Cut the sausage into small pieces.
4. Add oil to a skillet and allow to heat. Add eggs and sausage pieces and season with salt and pepper. Cook for about 3 minutes.
5. Spoon a spoonful of mixture into the growing triangles of dough and roll to seal.
6. Bake in air fryer until golden brown, about 5 minutes. Serve immediately.

PER SERVING

Calories 350 | Protein 11g | Carbs 23g

Spicy Green Beans

Prep time: 10 minutes | Cook time: 25 minutes | Serves 4

- 12 ounces fresh green beans
- 1 teaspoon soy sauce
- 1 clove garlic, minced
- 1 tablespoon sesame oil
- 1 teaspoon rice wine vinegar
- ½ teaspoon red pepper flakes

1. Preheat air fryer to 400 °F.
2. Place green beans in a bowl, and then whisk together sesame oil, soy sauce, rice wine vinegar, and red pepper flakes.
3. Pour over green beans and toss to coat.
4. Let marinate for 5 minutes before you cook them in the air fryer.

PER SERVING

Calories: 59 | Fat: 3.6g | Carbs: 6.6g | Protein: 1.7g | Sugar: 1.3g | Sodium: 80mg

Brussels Hash

Prep time: 5 minutes | Cook time: 25 minutes | Serves 2

- 2 cloves of garlic, minced
- 4 eggs, beaten
- 1 lb. Brussels sprouts, cut into four pieces
- ½ teaspoon salt
- 6 slices of bacon, chopped, cooked
- ½ cup chopped white onion
- ½ teaspoon ground black pepper

1. Preheat air fryer to 360 degrees F.
2. In a bowl, mix bacon, Brussels sprouts, onion, garlic, salt, and pepper.
3. Pour the mixture into a frying pan and cook for 15 minutes.
4. Pour the beaten eggs into the basket and put the pan back into the air fryer to cook another 10 minutes.
5. Stir well to break up the hash and enjoy hot.

PER SERVING

Calories 198 | Protein 15g | Carbs 21g

Mushroom Oatmeal

Prep time: 10 minutes | Cook time: 25 minutes | Serves 4

- One small yellow onion, chopped
- 1 cup steel-cut oats
- 1 Garlic cloves, minced
- 2 Tablespoons butter
- ½ cup of water
- One and a half cup of canned chicken stock
- Thyme springs, chopped
- 2 Tablespoons extra virgin olive oil
- ½ cup gouda cheese, grated
- 1 cup mushroom, sliced
- Salt and black pepper to taste

1. Heat a pan over medium heat, which suits your air fryer with the butter, add onions and garlic, stir and cook for 4 minutes.
2. Add oats, sugar, salt, pepper, stock, and thyme, stir, place in the air fryer and cook for 16 minutes at 360 F.
3. In the meantime, prepare a skillet over medium heat with the olive oil, add mushrooms, cook them for 3 minutes, add oatmeal and cheese, whisk, divide into bowls and serve for breakfast.

PER SERVING

Calories: 283.7 | Protein: 17.5g | Carbs: 19.6g | Fat: 7.5g

Green Beans and Potato Fry

Prep time: 10 minutes | Cook time: 12 minutes | Serves 2

- 1 cup potato cubes
- 1 small chopped onion
- 1 teaspoon coriander powder
- ¼ teaspoon garam masala powder
- ½ teaspoon ginger garlic paste
- 1 teaspoon lime juice
- 1.5 cups chopped green beans
- ½ teaspoon turmeric powder
- ½ teaspoon red chili powder
- salt to taste
- 1 teaspoon oil

1. Wash the vegetables in running water and cut them. Mix all the vegetables with all the spices and oil in a large bowl.
2. Put parchment paper on the air fryer basket as a lining.
3. Arrange the vegetables on top of the parchment paper so that they won't burn.
4. Then put them in your air fryer and cook for about 10-12 minutes, until done.
5. Stir them occasionally to make sure even cooking. It should turn to a golden brown color when done cooking.
6. Remove them from the air fryer when they are done; sprinkle some lime juice over the top and garnish with cilantro leaves (optional).
7. Enjoy them with some dinner!

PER SERVING

Calories: 80Kcal | Fat: 2g | Carbs: 14g | Protein: 4g | Sugar: 7g | Sodium: 10mg

Bacon and Cheese Rolls

Prep time: 8 to minutes | Cook time: 10 minutes | Serves 4

- 1 lb. cheddar cheese, grated
- 1 lb. bacon rashers
- 1 8 oz. can Pillsbury Crescent dough

1. Warm up the Air Fryer to 330°F.
2. Cut the bacon rashers across into ¼ inch strips and mix with the cheddar cheese. Set aside.
3. Cut the dough sheet to 1 by 1.5 inches pieces. Place an equal amount of bacon and cheese mixture on the center of the dough pieces and pinch corners together to enclose stuffing.
4. Transfer the parcels in the Air Fry basket and bake for 7 minutes at 330°F.
5. Increase the temperature to 390°F and bake for another 3 minutes. Serve warm.

PER SERVING

Calories 231.3| Fat 7.4 g | Carbs: 5.5 g| Protein 13.3 g

Sausage and Zucchini

Prep time: 5 minutes | Cook time: 30 minutes | Serves 4

- 10 eggs
- ½ cup almond flour
- 1 cup grated cheddar cheese
- 2 tsp baking powder
- 4 cups grated zucchini
- 1 tsp salt
- ½ pound light cream cheese
- ½ tsp ground black pepper

1. Preheat the deep fryer to 350 degrees F. Line a baking sheet with parchment paper.
2. Whisk together the almond flour, baking powder, salt and pepper. Place the light cream cheese in another bowl and beat with eggs. Beat until the mixture is smooth.
3. Now incorporate the zucchini into the cream cheese and mix. Add the almond mixture to the bowl of cream cheese and mix well. Add the cheddar cheese as well.
4. In the prepared pan initially pour the mixture and cook in the air fryer for 30 minutes. Allow to cool slightly before serving.

PER SERVING

Calories 280 | Protein 17g | Carbs 23g

Breakfast Potatoes

Prep time: 5 minutes | Cook time: 20 minutes | Serves 6

- 3 bite-sized cut potatoes
- ½ diced bell pepper
- 1 teaspoon garlic powder
- 1 teaspoon onion powder
- salt and pepper (to taste)
- 1 tablespoon extra virgin olive oil
- parsley

1. To make Air-Fried Breakfast Potatoes, preheat the air fryer to 380°F.
2. Then wash and scrub the potatoes and cut them into bite-sized pieces with the skin on.
3. Pat them dry with paper towels, then transfer them to a large bowl.
4. Add spices; coat with olive oil, and stir to combine well.
5. Add bell pepper; stir to combine well (garnish with parsley for added color!).
6. Cook for 20 minutes or until the desired level of crispness. Shake and turn potatoes halfway through cook time to ensure even browning (shaking may cause chips to sizzle).

PER SERVING

Calories: 111Kcal | Fat: 2g | Carbs: 21g | Protein: 3g | Sugar: 1g | Sodium: 782mg

Breakfast Sandwiches

Prep time: 5 minutes | Cook time:8 minutes |Serves 1

- 4 mini bagels, sliced
- 4 veggie sausage patties
- 4 slices soy cheese
- 1 avocado, sliced

1. Set the air fryer temp to 400°F.
2. Place the bagels cut side up and the sausage patties in the fryer basket. Cook until the bagels are toasted, about 4 minutes.
3. Pause the machine and remove the bagels. Set aside.
4. Top each patty with 1 slice of cheese. Restart the machine and cook for 4 minutes more.
5. Transfer each patty to between 2 bagel halves. Top each patty with avocado slices and serve immediately.

PER SERVING

Calories: 352 | Fat: 16g | Sat Fat: 4g | Cholesterol:0mg | Sodium: 633mg | Carbohydrates 29g | Fiber:8g | Sugar:3g | Protein:17g

Grilled Cheese Sandwiches

Prep time: 2 minutes | Cook time: 7 minutes | Serves 2

- 4 slices American cheese
- 4 slices sandwich bread
- Pat Butter

1. Warm your air fryer to 360°F. Fill the center of 2 bread slices with two slices of American cheese.
2. Binge an even layer of butter on each side of the sandwich and position it in the hamper of your air fryer in a single layer. Insert toothpicks on the corners of each sandwich to seal.
3. Air-fries the sandwiches for 4 minutes, flipping once, and cook for another 3 minutes until toasted.

PER SERVING

Calories: 296.8 | Fat: 14.4g | Carbs: 30.7g | Fiber: 1g, Sugar: 6.8g | Protein: 12.1g

Chapter 4
Snacks and Appetizers

Air Fryer Squash

Prep time: 5 minutes | Cook time: 10 minutes | Serves 4

- Olive oil: 1/2 Tablespoon
- One squash
- Salt: 1/2 teaspoon
- Rosemary: 1/2 teaspoon

1. Chop the squash in slices of 1/4 thickness. Discard the seeds.
2. In a bowl, add olive oil, salt, rosemary with squash slices. Mix well.
3. Cook the squash for ten minutes at 400 ° F. Flip the squash halfway through. Make sure it is cooked completely.

PER SERVING

Calories: 67.4 | Protein: 1.4g | Carbs: 8.4g | Fat: 3.7g

Black Bean Quesadillas

Prep time: 10 minutes | Cook time:10 minutes | Serves 2

- 8 small flour tortillas (regular or whole grain)
- 1½ cups shredded vegan Cheddar-style or mozzarella-style cheese
- 1 cup canned black beans, drained and rinsed
- ½ cup chopped fresh cilantro
- Salsa

1. Set the air fryer temp to 380°F.
2. In the center of each tortilla, place an equal amount of cheese, beans, and cilantro. Fold the tortillas in half.
3. Working in batches, place 4 tortillas in the fryer basket and cook until the cheese has melted and the tops are golden and crispy, about 4 to 5 minutes.
4. Transfer the quesadillas to a platter and serve immediately with the salsa.

PER SERVING

Calories: 347 | Fat: 11g | Sat Fat: 6g | Cholesterol:0mg | Sodium: 651mg | Carbohydrates 52g | Fiber:5g | Sugar:1g | Protein:10g

Asparagus Tips

Prep time: 2 minutes | Cook time:5 minutes | Serves 2

- 1 large bunch of asparagus
- 2 tsp olive oil
- ¼ tsp kosher salt
- ¼ tsp freshly ground black pepper
- juice of ½ lemon

1. Set the air fryer temp to 380°F.
2. Remove and discard the tough ends of the asparagus stalks. Chop the stalks into 1-inch (2.5cm) pieces.
3. In a large bowl, combine the asparagus, olive oil, salt, and pepper. Toss well to coat.
4. Place the asparagus in the fryer basket and cook for 5 minutes or until they reach your desired doneness.
5. Transfer the asparagus to a serving bowl. Add the lemon juice and toss well to coat before serving.

PER SERVING

Calories: 27 | Fat: 0g | Sat Fat: 0g | Cholesterol:0mg | Sodium: 293mg | Carbohydrates 5g | Fiber:3g | Sugar:3g | Protein:3

Herb Vegetables

Prep time: 10 minutes | Cook time:18 minutes | Serves 4

- 1 Red Bell Pepper, Sliced
- 8 Ounces Mushrooms, Sliced
- 1 cup Green Beans
- 3 Cloves Garlic, Sliced
- 1/3 Cup Red Onion, Diced
- 1 Teaspoon Olive Oil
- 1/2 Teaspoon Basil
- 1/2 Teaspoon Tarragon

1. Chopped green beans into two-inch pieces
2. Get out a bowl and mix your red onion, red bell pepper, mushrooms, garlic, and green beans.
3. Drizzle your olive oil next, making sure everything is mixed and coasted. Add in your herbs and toss again.
4. Place them in your air fryer basket, and roast until tender. This will take fourteen to eighteen minutes.
5. Serve warm.

PER SERVING

Calories:44 | Fat:2g | Carbohydrates: 5g | Protein: 2.5g

Sesame Broccoli

Prep time: 2 minutes | Cook time:6 minutes | Serves 6

- 6 cups broccoli florets
- 1 tbsp sesame oil
- 1 tsp kosher salt
- 2 tsp sesame seeds, plus more

1. Set the air fryer temp to 400°F.
2. In a large bowl, combine the broccoli, sesame oil, and salt. Toss well to coat.
3. Place the broccoli in the fryer basket and cook for 5 minutes. Pause the machine and add the sesame seeds. Restart the machine and cook for 1 minute more.
4. Transfer the broccoli to a platter. Sprinkle more sesame seeds over the top before serving.

PER SERVING

Calories: 57 | Fat: 3g | Sat Fat: 0g | Cholesterol:0mg | Sodium: 418mg | Carbohydrates 6g | Fiber:3g | Sugar:1g | Protein:3g

---

Garlic Kale Chips

Prep time: 6–7 minutes | Cook time: 5 minutes | Serves 2

- 1 tbsp. yeast flakes
- Sea salt to taste
- 4 cups packed kale
- 2 tbsp. olive oil
- 1 tsp. garlic, minced
- ½ cup ranch seasoning pieces

1. In a bowl, place the oil, kale, garlic, and ranch seasoning pieces. Add the yeast and mix well. Dump the coated kale into an air fryer basket and cook at 375°F for 5 minutes.
2. Shake after 3 minutes and serve.

PER SERVING

Calories 51| Fat 1.7g| Carbs 9.9g|Protein 46.3g

Brussels Sprouts

Prep time: 5 minutes | Cook time:10 minutes | Serves 4

- Almonds sliced: 1/4 cup
- Brussel sprouts: 2 cups
- Kosher salt
- Parmesan cheese: 1/4 cup grated
- Olive oil: 2 Tablespoons
- Everything bagel seasoning: 2 Tablespoons

1. In a saucepan, add Brussel sprouts with two cups of water and let it cook over medium flame for almost ten minutes.
2. Strain sprouts and cut them in half.
3. In a mixing bowl, add sliced brussels sprout with crushed almonds, oil, salt, parmesan cheese, and everything bagel seasoning.
4. Completely coat the sprouts.
5. Cook in the air fryer for 12-15 minutes at 375 F or until light brown.
6. Serve hot.

PER SERVING

Calories:155 | Fat:3g |Carbohydrates: 3g | Protein: 6g

Lentil Enchiladas

Prep time: 15 minutes | Cook time:10 minutes | Serves 1

- 2 cups cooked lentils
- ½ white onion, diced
- 3 tbsp chopped fresh cilantro
- 2 medium corn tortillas
- ½ cup salsa verde
- ½ cup shredded vegan Cheddar-style cheese

1. Set the air fryer temp to 380°F. Spray a baking dish with nonstick cooking spray.
2. In a medium bowl, combine the lentils, onion, and cilantro. Spoon an equal amount of the mixture into the center of each tortilla and roll them up. Place the tortillas in the dish and top with the salsa verde and cheese.
3. Place the dish in the fryer basket and cook until the edges are golden brown and the cheese has melted, about 10 minutes.
4. Remove the dish from the fryer basket and allow the enchiladas to cool slightly before serving.

PER SERVING

Calories: 342 | Fat: 4g | Sat Fat: 1g | Cholesterol:0mg | Sodium: 735mg | Carbohydrates 59g | Fiber:19g | Sugar:6g | Protein:21g

Lamb Chops with Mint

Prep time: 10 minutes | Cook time: 40 minutes | Serves 6

- 4 cups spinach
- 5 tablespoons lemon juice
- 1 tablespoon chopped fresh mint
- 5 tablespoons olive oil
- ¼ teaspoon ground black pepper
- ½ tablespoon sea salt
- 2 pounds lamb chops
- 2 zucchini, thinly sliced

1. Preheat the air fryer to 340 degrees F and prepare the air fryer tray with a piece of aluminum foil.
2. In a bowl, combine mint, four tablespoons olive oil, and lemon juice. Add lamb chops to the bowl and toss to coat. Cover the bowl and refrigerate for 1 hour.
3. Over high heat, in a skillet, add the remaining tablespoon of olive oil to brown the marinated lamb chops on each side for 5 minutes.
4. Move the browned pork lamb to the prepared, foil-lined tray and pour the marinade over the ribs. Add the zucchini and spinach, arranging them on top of and around the lamb chops.
5. Place the tray in the preheated air fryer for 30 minutes. Serve hot.

PER SERVING

Calories 230 | Protein 24g | Carbs 9g

Hasselback Sweet Potatoes

Prep time: 3 minutes | Cook time:20 minutes |Serves 1

- 4 medium Hasselback sweet potatoes
- 4 tsp olive oil
- 1 tsp kosher salt
- ½ tsp freshly ground black pepper

1. Set the air fryer temp to 300°F.
2. Use a fork to poke a few holes in each sweet potato. Microwave the sweet potatoes for 3 minutes.
3. Use a sharp knife to make a series of ⅛-inch (3mm) slices along the top of each potato. Go only two-thirds of the way down so the potato remains in one piece.
4. Drizzle each potato with 1 teaspoon of olive oil. Season each with ½ teaspoon of salt and ¼ teaspoon of pepper.
5. Place the sweet potatoes in the fryer basket and bake until tender and the tops are crispy, about 20 minutes.
6. Transfer the potatoes to a platter and allow to cool slightly before serving.

PER SERVING

Calories: 160 | Fat: 4g | Sat Fat: 1g | Cholesterol:0mg | Sodium: 432mg | Carbohydrates 33g | Fiber:4g | Sugar:7g | Protein:2g

Caprese Rollups

Prep time: 10 minutes | Cook time: 15 minutes | Serves 8

- 2 tablespoons chopped fresh basil
- 5 ounces of mozzarella, sliced
- 3 tablespoons olive oil
- 2 tomatoes
- 1 zucchini, thinly sliced lengthwise

1. Preheat your deep fryer to 340 degrees F and place baking paper on a baking sheet.
2. Lay out the zucchini slices, place a piece of tomato, cheese, and basil on each zucchini slice, then roll up to enclose the filling. Secure with a toothpick and then put on a baking sheet lined with baking paper.
3. Drizzle with olive oil and place in the fryer to cook for 15 minutes. Serve warm.

PER SERVING

Calories 67 | Protein 5g | Carbs 8g

Broccoli Salad

Prep time: 5 minutes | Cook time: 25 minutes | Serves 6

- ½ teaspoon Dijon mustard
- ½ teaspoon kosher salt
- 2 teaspoons chopped fresh rosemary
- 1 teaspoon maple extract
- ¼ teaspoon dried sage
- 1 pound chopped broccoli florets
- ½ cup olive oil

1. Preheat the air fryer to 370 degrees F and line the air fryer tray with foil.
2. Combine the chopped broccoli with sage, rosemary, and olive oil.
3. Cook in the air fryer for 25 minutes.
4. Place cooked broccoli in a bowl and add remaining ingredients to make a dressing. Mix well and serve.

PER SERVING

Calories 241 | Protein 3g | Carbs 11g

Crisp Broccoli

Prep time: 10 minutes | Cook time:14 minutes |Serves 4

- 1 Tablespoon Lemon Juice, Fresh
- 2 Teaspoon Olive Oil
- 1 Head Broccoli

1. Start by rinsing your broccoli and patting it dry.
2. Cut it into florets, and then separate them. Make sure that if you use the stems, it's cut into one-inch chunks and peeled.
3. Toss your broccoli pieces with your lemon juice and olive oil until they're well coated.
4. Roast your broccoli in batches for ten for fourteen minutes each. They should be tender and crisp.
5. Serve warm.

PER SERVING

Calories:90 | Fat:0.5g |Carbohydrates: 7g | Protein: 9g

Spiced Nuts

Prep time: 7 minutes | Cook time: 25 minutes | Serves 3

- 1 cup almonds
- 1 cup pecan halves
- 1 cup cashews
- 1 egg white, beaten
- ½ tsp. cinnamon, ground
- Pinch cayenne pepper
- ¼ tsp. cloves, ground
- Pinch salt

1. Combine the egg white with spices. Preheat your air fryer to 300°F.
2. Toss the nuts in the spiced mixture. Cook for 25 minutes, stirring throughout cooking time.

PER SERVING

Calories: 88.3 | Fat: 7.4g | Carbs: 3.7g | Protein: 2.4g

Roasted Bell Pepper

Prep time: 10 minutes | Cook time:20 minutes |Serves 4

- 1 Teaspoon Olive Oil
- 1/2 Teaspoon Thyme
- 4 Cloves Garlic, Minced
- 4 Bell Peppers, Cut into Fourths

1. Start by putting your peppers in your basket and drizzling them with olive oil. Make sure they're coated well and then roast for fifteen minutes.
2. Sprinkle with thyme and garlic, roasting for an additional three to five minutes. They should be tender and serve warm.

PER SERVING

Calories:74 | Fat:4g |Carbohydrates: 9g | Protein: 1g

Tempeh & Walnut Tacos

Prep time: 10 minutes | Cook time:20 minutes |Serves 2

- 2 tsp canola oil
- ¼ tsp ground cumin
- ½ tsp kosher salt
- ½ tsp chili powder
- 8oz (225g) tempeh, diced
- ¾ cup chopped walnuts
- ⅓ cup mild salsa (Green Mountain Gringo recommended)
- For Serving
- 8 small corn tortillas, warmed
- chopped romaine or iceberg lettuce
- guacamole

1. Set the air fryer temp to 330°F.
2. In a medium bowl, combine the canola oil, cumin, salt, and chili powder. Add the tempeh and toss well to coat.
3. Place the tempeh in the fryer basket and cook for 10 minutes. Pause the machine to add the walnuts and shake the basket gently to toss them with the tempeh. Restart the machine and cook for 5 to 10 minutes more.
4. Transfer the tempeh and walnuts to a clean medium bowl. Add the salsa and toss well to coat.
5. Place the tempeh and walnut mixture in the tortillas. Serve with the lettuce and guacamole.

PER SERVING

Calories: 325 | Fat: 15g | Sat Fat: 2g | Cholesterol:0mg | Sodium: 380mg | Carbohydrates 38g | Fiber:8g | Sugar:3g | Protein:12g

Cheesy Chicken Omelet

Prep time: 5 minutes | Cook time: 18 minutes | Serves 2

- Cooked Chicken Breast: half cup (diced)
- Four eggs
- Onion powder: 1/4 tsp
- Salt: 1/2 tsp.
- Pepper: 1/4 tsp.
- Shredded cheese: 2 tbsp.
- Garlic powder: 1/4 tsp.

1. Take two ramekins, grease with olive oil. Divided all ingredients in 2 portions.
2. Add two eggs to each ramekin. Add cheese, onion powder, salt, pepper, garlic and blend to combine. Add 1/4 cup of cooked chicken on top.
3. Cook at 330 °F for 14-18 minutes in the air fryer.

PER SERVING

Calories: 184.6 | Protein: 19.5g | Carbs: 8.7g | Fat: 4.7g

Vegetable Spring Rolls

Prep time: 10 minutes | Cook time:15 minutes |Serves 4

- Toasted sesame seeds
- Large carrots – grated
- Spring roll wrappers
- One egg white
- Gluten-free soy sauce, a dash
- Half cabbage: sliced
- Olive oil: 2 tbsp.

1. In a pan over high flame heat, 2 tbsp of oil and sauté the chopped vegetables. Then add soy sauce. Do not overcook the vegetables.
2. Turn off the heat and add toasted sesame seeds.
3. Lay spring roll wrappers flat on a surface and add egg white with a brush on the sides.
4. Add some vegetable mix in the wrapper and fold.
5. Spray oil in spring rolls and air fry for 8 minutes at 200 C.
6. Serve with dipping sauce.

PER SERVING

Calories:129 | Fat:16.3g |Carbohydrates: 8.2g | Protein: 12.1g

Avocado Fries

Prep time: 10 minutes | Cook time:10 minutes |Serves 2

- One avocado
- One egg
- Whole wheat breadcrumbs: 1/2 cup
- Salt: 1/2 teaspoon

1. Avocado should be firm and firm. Cut into wedges.
2. In a bowl, beat the egg with salt. In another bowl, add the crumbs.
3. Coat wedges in egg, then in crumbs.
4. Air fry them at 400 F for 8-10 minutes. Toss halfway through.
5. Serve hot.

PER SERVING

Calories:251 | Fat:17g |Carbohydrates: 19g | Protein: 6g

French Fries

Prep time: 7 minutes | Cook time: 20 minutes | Serves 4

- 1 large rutabaga, peeled, cut into spears about ¼-inch wide
- Salt and pepper to taste
- ½ tsp. paprika
- 2 tbsp. coconut oil

1. Preheat your air fryer to 450°F. Mix the oil, paprika, salt, and pepper.
2. Pour the oil mixture over the rutabaga. Cook in the air fryer for 20 minutes or until crispy.

PER SERVING

Calories: 112 | Fat: 7.1g | Carbs: 12.3g | Protein: 1.8g

Chapter 5
Poultry

Lemon-Garlic Chicken

Prep time: 2 hours | Cook time: 35 minutes | Serves 4

- Lemon juice ¼ cup
- 1 Tbsp. olive oil
- 1 tsp mustard
- Cloves of garlic
- ¼ tsp salt
- ⅛ tsp black pepper
- Chicken thighs
- Lemon wedges

1. In a bowl, whisk together the olive oil, lemon juice, mustard Dijon, garlic, salt, and pepper.
2. Place the chicken thighs in a large ziploc bag. Spill marinade over chicken & seal bag, ensuring all chicken parts are covered. Cool for at least 2 hours.
3. Preheat a frying pan to 360 F. Remove the chicken with towels from the marinade, & pat dry.
4. Place pieces of chicken in the air fryer basket, if necessary, cook them in batches.
5. Fry till chicken is no longer pink on the bone & the juices run smoothly, 22 to 24 min. Upon serving, press a lemon slice across each piece.

PER SERVING

Calories: 257.5 | Protein: 19.9g | Carbs: 3.1g | Fat: 18.1g

Ginger and Coconut Chicken

Prep time:5 minutes |Cook time: 20 minutes |Serves 4

- 4 chicken breasts, skinless, boneless and halved
- 4 tablespoons coconut aminos
- 1 teaspoon olive oil
- 2 tablespoons stevia
- Salt and black pepper to the taste
- ¼ cup chicken stock
- 1 tablespoon ginger, grated

1. In a pan that fits the air fryer, combine the chicken with the ginger and all the ingredients and toss..
2. Put the pan in your air fryer and cook at 4380 degrees F for 20, shaking the fryer halfway.
3. Divide between plates and serve with a side salad.

PER SERVING

Calories 256| Fat 12| Fiber 4| Carbs 6| Protein 14

"Fried" BBQ Sauce Chicken

Prep time: 10 minutes | Cook time: 15 minutes | Serves 4

- 2 eggs
- ½ cup grated parmesan
- ½ cup whole milk
- 1 pound chicken tenders
- ¼ cup whey protein powder
- ¼ tsp ground black pepper
- ¼ tsp salt
- 2 Tbsp olive oil

- ½ cup keto BBQ sauce
- ½ tsp paprika

1. Preheat the fryer to 450 degrees F and place aluminum foil on the tray.
2. Place chicken tenders and whole milk in a bowl. Cover the bowl and marinate in the refrigerator overnight. In a bowl, mix together the parmesan cheese, protein powder, salt, pepper and paprika. In another bowl, beat the egg.
3. Dip the chicken into the egg and then into the prepared protein mixture.
4. Place the chicken bites on the baking sheet and drizzle with the olive oil.
5. Cook for about 15 minutes in the air fryer. Serve with BBQ sauce. Enjoy immediately!

PER SERVING

Calories 390 | Protein 15g | Carbs 30g

Garlic Chicken Wings

Prep time:5 minutes |Cook time: 30 minutes |Serves 4

- 2 pounds chicken wings
- ¼ cup olive oil
- Juice of 2 lemons
- Zest of 1 lemon, grated Apinch of salt and black pepper
- 2 garlic cloves, minced

1. In a bowl, mix the chicken wings with the rest of the ingredients and toss well.
2. Put the chicken wings in your air fryer's basket and cook at 400 degrees F for 30 minutes, shaking halfway.
3. Divide between plates and serve with a side salad.

PER SERVING

Calories 263| Fat 14| Fiber 4| Carbs 6| Protein 15

Rolls Stuffed with Broccoli and Carrots with Chicken

Prep time: 15 minutes | Cook time:25 minutes |Serves 4

- 8 sheets of rice pasta
- 1 chicken breast
- 1 onion
- 1 carrot
- 150g broccolis
- 1 can of sweet corn
- Extra virgin olive oil
- Salt
- Ground pepper
- Soy sauce
- 1 bag of rice three delicacies

1. Start with the vegetable that you have to cook previously, stop them, peel the carrot.
2. Cut the carrot and broccoli as small as you can. Add the broccolis and the carrot to a pot with boiling water and cook a few minutes, they have to be tender, but not too much, that crunch a little.
3. Drain well and reserve. Cut the onion into julienne. Cut the breast into strips.
4. In the Wok, put some extra virgin olive oil.
5. Add to the wok when it is hot, the onion and the chicken breast. Sauté well until the chicken is cooked.
6. Drain the corn and add to the wok along with the broccolis and the carrot.
7. Sauté so that the ingredients are mixed. Add salt, ground pepper and a little soy sauce.
8. Mix well and let the filling cool. Hydrate the rice pasta sheets.
9. Spread on the worktable and distribute the filling between the sheets of rice paste.
10. Assemble the rolls and paint with a little oil.
11. Put in the air fryer, those who enter do not pile up. Select 10 minutes 200 degrees C.
12. Select 180 degrees C, 5 minutes.
13. Make while the rice as indicated by the manufacturer in its bag.
14. Serve the rice with the rolls.

PER SERVING

Calories:125 | Fat:4.58g |Carbohydrates: 16.83g | Protein: 4.69g

Pickled Poultry

Prep time: 10 minutes | Cook time:25 minutes |Serves 4

- 600g of poultry, without bones or skin
- 3 white onions, peeled and cut into thin slices
- 5 garlic cloves, peeled and sliced
- 3 dl olive oil
- 1 dl apple cider vinegar
- 1/2 l white wine
- 2 bay leaves
- 5 g peppercorns
- Flour
- Pepper
- Salt

1. Rub the bird in dice that we will pepper and flour
2. Put oil in the prepared pan and heat. When the oil is hot, fry the floured meat dice in it until golden brown.
3. Take them out and reserve, placing them in a clay or oven dish. Strain the oil in which you have fried the meat
4. Preheat the oven to 170° C
5. Put the already cast oil in another pan over the fire. Sauté the garlic and onions in it. Add the white wine and let cook about 3 minutes.
6. Remove the pan from the heat, add the vinegar to the oil and wine. Remove, rectify salt, and pour this mixture into the source where you had left the bird dice.
7. Put in the oven, lower the temperature to 140°C and bake for 1 and 1/2 hours. Remove the source from the oven and let it stand at room temperature
8. When the source is cold, put it in the fridge and let it rest a few hours before serving.

PER SERVING

Calories:232 | Fat:15g |Carbohydrates: 5.89g | Protein: 18.2g

Chili Pepper Duck Bites
Prep time:15 minutes |Cook time: 15 minutes |Serves 4

- 8 oz duck breast, skinless, boneless
- 1 teaspoon Erythritol
- ½ teaspoon salt
- 1 teaspoon chili pepper
- 1 tablespoon butter, softened
- ½ teaspoon minced garlic
- ½ teaspoon dried dill

1. Cut the duck breast into small pieces (bites).
2. Then sprinkle them with salt, chili pepper, Erythritol, dried dill, and minced garlic.
3. Leave the duck pieces for 10-15 minutes to marinate.
4. Meanwhile, preheat the air fryer to 365F.
5. Sprinkle the duck bites with butter and put in the air fryer.
6. Cook the duck bites for 10 minutes.
7. Then shake them well and cook for 5 minutes more at 400F.

PER SERVING

Calories 100| Fat 5.2| Fiber 0.1| Carbs 0.3| Protein 12.6

Buttery Chicken Wings
Prep time:5 minutes |Cook time: 30 minutes |Serves 4

- 2 pounds chicken wings
- Salt and black pepper to the taste
- 3 garlic cloves, minced
- 3 tablespoons butter, melted
- ½ cup heavy cream
- ½ teaspoon basil, dried
- ½ teaspoon oregano, dried
- ¼ cup parmesan, grated

1. In a baking dish that fits your air fryer, mix the chicken wings with all the ingredients except the parmesan and toss.
2. Put the dish to your air fryer and cook at 380 degrees F for 30 minutes.
3. Sprinkle the cheese on top, leave the mix aside for 10 minutes, divide between plates and serve.

PER SERVING

calories 270| fat 12| fiber 3| carbs 6| protein 17

Spicy Chicken Strips
Prep time: 5 minutes | Cook time:12 minutes |Serves 5

- 1 cup buttermilk
- 1 1/2 tbsp hot pepper sauce
- 1 tsp salt
- 1/2 tsp black pepper, divided
- 1 pound boneless and skinless chicken breasts
- 3/4 cup panko breadcrumbs
- 1/2 tsp salt
- 1/4 tsp hot pepper, or to taste
- 1 tbsp olive oil

1. Cut the boneless chicken breast into 3/4-inch strips
2. Put the buttermilk, hot sauce, salt and 1/4 teaspoon of black pepper in shallow bowl.
3. Put the chicken strips and refrigerate for at least two hours. Put breadcrumbs, salt, and the remaining black pepper and hot pepper in another bowl; Add and stir the oil.
4. Get the chicken strips from the marinade and discard the marinade.
5. Put the strips, few at the same time, to the crumb mixture. Press the crumbs to the strips to achieve a uniform and firm cover.
6. Put half of the strips in single layer inside the basket. Cook at 350F for 12 minutes. Cook the rest when the first batch is cooked.

PER SERVING

Calories:207 | Fat:9g |Carbohydrates: 5g | Protein: 25g

Turkey and Coconut Broccoli
Prep time:5 minutes |Cook time: 25 minutes |Serves 4

- 1 pound turkey meat, ground
- 2 garlic cloves, minced
- 1 teaspoon ginger, grated
- 2 teaspoons coconut aminos
- 3 tablespoons olive oil
- 2 broccoli heads, florets separated and then halved Apinch of salt and black pepper
- 1 teaspoon chili paste

1. Heat up a pan that fits the air fryer with the oil over medium heat, add the meat and brown for 5 minutes.
2. Add the rest of the ingredients, toss, put the pan in the fryer and cook at 380 degrees F for 20 minutes.
3. Divide everything between plates and serve.

PER SERVING

Calories 274| Fat 11| Fiber 3| Carbs 6| Protein 12

Thyme and Okra Chicken Thighs
Prep time:5 minutes |Cook time: 30 minutes |Serves 4

- 4 chicken thighs, bone-in and skinless Apinch of salt and black pepper
- 1 cup okra
- ½ cup butter, melted
- Zest of 1 lemon, grated
- 4 garlic cloves, minced
- 1 tablespoon thyme, chopped
- 1 tablespoon parsley, chopped

1. Heat up a pan that fits your air fryer with half of the butter over medium heat, add the chicken thighs and brown them for 2-3 minutes on each side.
2. Add the rest of the butter, the okra and all the remaining ingredients, toss, put the pan in the air fryer and cook at 370 degrees F for 20 minutes.
3. Divide between plates and serve.

PER SERVING

Calories 270| Fat 12| Fiber 4| Carbs 6| Protein 14

Lemon and Chili Chicken Drumsticks
Prep time:10 minutes |Cook time: 20 minutes |Serves 6

- 6 chicken drumsticks
- 1 teaspoon dried oregano
- 1 tablespoon lemon juice
- ½ teaspoon lemon zest, grated
- 1 teaspoon ground cumin
- ½ teaspoon chili flakes
- 1 teaspoon garlic powder
- ½ teaspoon ground coriander
- 1 tablespoon avocado oil

1. Rub the chicken drumsticks with dried oregano, lemon juice, lemon zest, ground cumin, chili flakes, garlic powder, and ground coriander.
2. Then sprinkle them with avocado oil and put in the air fryer.
3. Cook the chicken drumsticks for 20 minutes at 375F.

PER SERVING

Calories 85| Fat 3.1| Fiber 0.3| Carbs 0.9| Protein 12.9

Dill Chicken Fritters

Prep time:20 minutes |Cook time: 16 minutes |Serves 8

- 1-pound chicken breast, skinless, boneless
- 3 oz coconut flakes
- 1 tablespoon ricotta cheese
- 1 teaspoon mascarpone
- 1 teaspoon dried dill
- ½ teaspoon salt
- 1 egg yolk
- 1 teaspoon avocado oil

1. Cut the chicken breast into the tiny pieces and put them in the bowl.
2. Add coconut flakes, ricotta cheese, mascarpone, dried dill, salt, and egg yolk.
3. Then make the chicken fritters with the help of the fingertips.
4. Preheat the air fryer to 360F.
5. Line the air fryer basket with baking paper and put the chicken cakes in the air fryer.
6. Sprinkle the chicken fritters with avocado oil and cook for 8 minutes.
7. Then flip the chicken fritters on another side and cook them for 8 minutes more.

PER SERVING

Calories 114| Fat 5.9| Fiber 1| Carbs 1.9| Protein 13.1

Turkey and Chili Kale

Prep time:5 minutes |Cook time: 25 minutes |Serves 4

- 1 pound turkey meat, ground Apinch of salt and black pepper
- 2 tablespoons olive oil
- 1 teaspoon coconut aminos
- 2 spring onions, minced
- 4 cups kale, chopped
- 1 tablespoon garlic, chopped
- 1 red chili pepper, chopped
- ½ cup chicken stock

1. Heat up a pan that fits your air fryer with the oil over medium heat, add the meat, salt, pepper, spring onions and the garlic, stir and sauté for 5 minutes.
2. Add the rest of the ingredients, toss, put the pan in the fryer and cook at 380 degrees F for 20 minutes.
3. Divide between plates and serve

PER SERVING

Calories 261| Fat 12| Fiber 2| Carbs 5| Protein 13

Chicken with Mixed Vegetables
Prep time: 10 minutes | Cook time: 10 minutes | Serves 2

- 1/2 onion diced
- Chicken breast: 4 cups, cubed pieces
- Half zucchini chopped
- Italian seasoning: 1 tablespoon
- Bell pepper chopped: 1/2 cup
- Clove of garlic pressed
- Broccoli florets: 1/2 cup
- Olive oil: 2 tablespoons
- Half teaspoon of chili powder, garlic powder, pepper, salt

1. Let the air fryer heat to 400 F and dice the vegetables.
2. In a bowl, add the seasoning, oil and add vegetables, chicken and toss well.
3. Place chicken and vegetables in the air fryer, and cook for ten minutes, toss half way through, cook in batches.
4. Make sure the veggies are charred and the chicken is cooked through.
5. Serve hot.

PER SERVING

Calories: 229.6 | Protein: 26.5g | Carbs: 7.6g | Fat: 9.5g

Coconut-Crusted Turkey Fingers
Prep time: 20 minutes | Cook time: 10 minutes | Serves 4

- 1/2 pounds turkey breast tenderloins, cut into
- 1 tablespoon sesame seeds, toasted
- 1 teaspoon sesame oil
- 1/4 teaspoon salt
- 1/4 cup sweetened coconut, lightly toasted (shredded)
- 1/4 cup dry bread crumbs
- 1/2-inch strips 1 large egg white
- cooking spray

DIPPING SAUCE:
- 2/3 cup unsweetened pineapple juice
- grated lime zest and lime wedges
- 1/4 cup plum sauce
- 1/2 teaspoons prepared mustard
- 1/2 teaspoon cornstarch

1. To prepare the turkey, preheat the air fryer to 400°F. Whisk 2 egg whites and 2 tablespoons of oil in a shallow bowl.
2. In another shallow bowl, mix 4 teaspoons of coconut flour, 1 tablespoon of bread crumbs (preferably egg-free), 1 teaspoon of sesame seeds, and 1/4 teaspoon of salt.
3. Dip the turkey in this mixture, then into another mixture of 4 egg yolks, 1/2 cup water, and 2 tablespoons of oil. Pat this mixture onto the turkey so that it sticks well.
4. Finally, place your turkey in a single layer on greased trays in your air fryer basket.
5. Cook until golden brown – about 3-4 minutes – turning once or twice during cooking so that both sides get cooked evenly. Serve with grated lime zest for garnish if desired.

PER SERVING

Calories: 292Kcal | Fat: 9g | Carbs: 24g | Protein: 31g | Sugar: 5g | Sodium: 517mg

Buttermilk Fried Chicken

Prep time: 10 minutes | Cook time: 15 minutes | Serves 2

- ½ cup low-fat buttermilk
- 1/8 teaspoon hot sauce
- ½ pound boneless, skinless chicken breasts
- cooking spray
- 1/8 teaspoon salt
- 1/8 teaspoon coarse-ground black pepper
- 4 tablespoons corn flakes
- 2 tablespoons stone-ground cornmeal
- ½ teaspoon garlic powder
- 1 teaspoon paprika

1. Take a small mixing bowl, mix the buttermilk and hot sauce together. Place the chicken in the buttermilk mixture. Allow to stand for 15 minutes.
2. Place cornflakes into the work bowl of food processor. Process until coarse crumbs form. Add cornmeal, garlic powder, paprika, salt and pepper and pulse until evenly mixed. Pour crumbs into shallow bowl.
3. Coat chicken evenly in cornflake mixture; place pieces on wire rack.
4. Place the chicken in the air fryer basket and spray with nonstick cooking spray.
5. Cook for 7 minutes at 375°F, turning occasionally. Cook for an additional 7–10 minutes or until done and a meat thermometer inserted into the center registers 165°F.

PER SERVING

Calories: 160Kcal | Fat: 3.5g | Carbs: 7g | Protein: 24g | Sugar: 0g | Sodium: 190mg

Chicken Pizza

Prep time: 20 minutes | Cook time: 20 minutes | Serves 3

- 1 cup shredded cooked chicken
- 4 Tbsp fresh grated parmesan
- 1 Tbsp fresh chopped basil
- 1 cup almond flour
- 1 egg
- ½ cup fresh diced mozzarella
- 3 Tbsp water
- 1/3 cup keto buffalo sauce

1. Preheat the air fryer to 375 degrees F. Place aluminum foil on the tray of the air fryer.
2. Mix together the almond flour and water in a bowl. Add the egg and Parmesan cheese and knead.
3. When the dough is ready and soft place it on the prepared tray and with the help of a plate press into a ¼ inch thick circle.
4. In a bowl, mix the buffalo sauce and shredded chicken. Place the chicken mixture on top of the dough and top with mozzarella cheese and fresh basil.
5. Cook in the fryer for about 20 minutes or until the cheese is melted. Serve warm.

PER SERVING

Calories 380 | Protein 19g | Carbs 35g

Cream Cheese Chicken Mix

Prep time:15 minutes |Cook time: 16 minutes |Serves 4

- 1-pound chicken wings
- ¼ cup cream cheese
- 1 tablespoon apple cider vinegar
- 1 teaspoon Truvia
- ½ teaspoon smoked paprika
- ½ teaspoon ground nutmeg
- 1 teaspoon avocado oil

1. In the mixing bowl mix up cream cheese, Truvia, apple cider vinegar, smoked paprika, and ground nutmeg.
2. Then add the chicken wings and coat them in the cream cheese mixture well.
3. Leave the chicken winds in the cream cheese mixture for 10-15 minutes to marinate.
4. Meanwhile, preheat the air fryer to 380F.
5. Put the chicken wings in the air fryer and cook them for 8 minutes.
6. Then flip the chicken wings on another and brush with cream cheese marinade.
7. Cook the chicken wings for 8 minutes more.

PER SERVING

calories 271| fat 13.7| fiber 0.2| carbs 1.2| protein 34

Creamy Tomato Chicken

Prep time: 10 minutes | Cook time: 15 minutes | Serves 6

- ½ cup chicken broth
- 1 Tbsp tomato paste
- 1 ½ pounds chicken breast, thinly sliced
- 2 Tbsp olive oil
- 1 tsp garlic powder
- 2 cups baby spinach
- 1 tsp Italian seasoning
- ½ cup grated parmesan cheese
- ½ cup chopped sundried tomatoes
- 1 cup light cream

1. Preheat your air fryer to 375 degrees F. Prepare a baking sheet and insert aluminum foil.
2. Place the chicken drizzled with the olive oil in the baking dish and cook in the fryer for 5 minutes on each side.
3. In a bowl combine the remaining ingredients. Add all remaining ingredients to the pan, stirring briefly. Return the pan to the air fryer and cook for 10 minutes. Serve while hot!

PER SERVING

Calories 410 | Protein 15g | Carbs 24g

Bell Peppers Frittata
Prep time: 10 minutes | Cook time: 20 minutes | Serves 4

- 2 Tablespoons olive oil
- 2 cups chicken sausage, casings removed and chopped
- One sweet onion, chopped
- 1 red bell pepper, chopped
- 1 orange bell pepper, chopped
- 1 green bell pepper, chopped
- Salt and black pepper to taste
- 8 eggs, whisked
- ½ cup mozzarella cheese, shredded
- 2 teaspoons oregano, chopped

1. Add 1 spoonful of oil to the air fryer, add bacon, heat to 320 F, and brown for 1 minute.
2. Remove remaining butter, onion, red bell pepper, orange and white, mix and simmer for another 2 minutes.
3. Stir and cook for 15 minutes, add oregano, salt, pepper, and eggs.
4. Add mozzarella, leave frittata aside for a couple of minutes, divide and serve between plates.

PER SERVING
Calories: 211.6 | Protein: 12.6g | Carbs: 7.5g | Fat: 3.5g

Tasty Hassel Back Chicken
Prep time: 10 minutes | Cook time: 18 minutes | Serves 2

- 2 lbs chicken breasts, boneless and skinless
- ½ cup sauerkraut, squeezed and remove excess liquid
- 2 tbsp. thin Swiss cheese slices, tear into pieces
- 1 lbs thin deli corned beef slices, tear into pieces
- Salt and Pepper as per taste

1. Make five slits on top of chicken breasts. Season chicken with pepper and salt.
2. Stuff each slit with beef, sauerkraut, and cheese.
3. Spray chicken with cooking spray and place in the air fryer basket.
4. Cook chicken at 350°F for 18 minutes. Serve and enjoy.

PER SERVING
Calories: 723.2 | Fat: 39.1g | Carbs: 3.2g, Sugar 2.3g | Protein: 84.2g

Chapter 6
Red Meat

Air Fried Steak with Asparagus
Prep time: 20 minutes | Cook time: 30 minutes | Serves 2

- Olive oil spray
- Flank steak (2 pounds)- cut into 6 pieces
- Kosher salt and black pepper
- Two cloves of minced garlic
- Asparagus: 4 cups
- Tamari sauce: half cup
- Three bell peppers: sliced thinly
- Beef broth: 1/3 cup
- 1 Tbsp. of unsalted butter
- Balsamic vinegar: 1/4 cup

1. Sprinkle salt and pepper on steak and rub.
2. In a ziploc bag, add Tamari sauce and garlic, then add steak, toss well and seal the bag.
3. Let it marinate for one hour to overnight.
4. Place asparagus and bell peppers in the center of the steak.
5. Roll the steak around the vegetables and close it well with toothpicks.
6. Preheat the air fryer. Spray the steak with olive oil spray. and place steaks in the air fryer.
7. Cook for 15 minutes at 400°F.
8. Remove the steak from the air fryer and let it rest for five minute before slicing.
9. In the meantime, add balsamic vinegar, butter, and broth over medium flame. Mix well and reduce it by half. Add salt and pepper to taste. Pour over steaks right before serving.

PER SERVING

Calories: 469.5 | Protein: 29.6g | Carbs: 19.5g | Fat: 14.6g

Steak Fajitas
Prep time: 15 minutes | Cook time: 15 minutes | Serves 4

- 1/4 cup diced red onion
- 4 whole wheat tortillas, warmed
- 1/8 cup lime juice
- 1 teaspoon ground cumin, divided
- 1/2 jalapeno pepper, seeded and minced
- sliced avocado and lime wedges
- 2 tablespoons minced fresh cilantro
- 1 large tomato, seeded and chopped
- 1/4 teaspoon salt, divided
- 1/2 beef flank steak
- 1/2 large onion, halved and sliced

1. For salsa, mix first 5 ingredients (lemon juice, lime juice, onion, cumin, and salt) in a small bowl; let stand until serving. Meanwhile, sprinkle steak with the remaining cumin and salt; place on greased tray in air-fryer basket.
2. Cook until the internal temperature of the meat reaches desired doneness (for medium-rare, the reading should be 135°F; medium 140°F, medium-well 145°F), 6-8 minutes per side.
3. Remove from basket and let stand 5 minutes

before slicing thinly across the grain. Serve with onion and salsa.

PER SERVING

Calories: 309Kcal | Fat: 9g | Carbs: 29g | Protein: 27g | Sugar: 3g | Sodium: 498mg

Meatballs and Creamy Potatoes
Prep time: 45–50 minutes | Cook time: 35 minutes | Serves 4–6

- 12 oz. lean ground beef
- 1 medium onion, finely chopped
- 1 tbsp. parsley leaves, finely chopped
- ½ tbsp. fresh thyme leaves
- ½ tsp. minced garlic
- 2 tbsp olive oil
- 1 tsp. salt
- 1 tsp. ground black pepper
- 1 enormous egg
- 3 tbsp. bread crumbs
- 1 cup half & half, or ½ cup whole milk and ½ cup cream mixed
- 7 medium russet potatoes
- ½ tsp. ground nutmeg
- ½ cup grated gruyere cheese

1. Place the ground beef, onions, parsley, thyme, garlic, olive oil, salt and pepper, egg, and breadcrumbs in a bowl, and mix well. Place in refrigerator until needed.
2. In another bowl, place half & half and nutmeg, and whisk to combine.
3. Peel and wash potatoes, and then slice them thinly, ⅛ to 1/5 of an inch, if needed, to use a mandolin.
4. Warm up the Air Fryer to 390°F.
5. Place potato slices in a bowl with half & half and toss to coat well. Layer the potato slices in an Air Fryer baking accessory and pour over the leftover half & half. Bake for 25 minutes at 390°F.
6. Meanwhile, take the meat mixture out of the fridge and shape it into inch and half balls.
7. When potatoes are cooked, place meatballs on top of them in one layer and cover with the grated Gruyere.
8. Cook for another 10 minutes.

PER SERVING

Calories: 231.2 | Fat: 8g | Carbs: 5.8g | Protein: 12.8g

Pork Chops

Prep time: 10 minutes | Cook time: 15 minutes | Serves 4

- pork chops
- Pepper
- Salt

1. Season pork chops with pepper and salt.
2. Place the dehydrating tray in a multi-level air fryer basket and place the basket in the instant pot.
3. Place pork chops on dehydrating tray.
4. Seal pot with air fryer lid, set the temperature of the Air Fryer to 400°F and timer for 15 minutes. Turn pork chops halfway through.

PER SERVING

Calories: 255.6 | Fat: 19.3g | Carbs: 0g, Sugar 0g | Protein: 18.3g

Flavored Rib Eye Steak

Prep time: 10 minutes | Cook time:20 minutes |Serves 4

- 2 pounds rib eye steak
- Salt and black pepper to the taste
- 1 tablespoons olive oil
- For the rub:
- 3 tablespoons sweet paprika
- 2 tablespoons onion powder
- 2 tablespoons garlic powder
- 1 tablespoon brown sugar
- 2 tablespoons oregano, dried
- 1 tablespoon cumin, ground
- 1 tablespoon rosemary, dried

1. In a bowl, mix paprika with onion and garlic powder, sugar, oregano, rosemary, salt, pepper, and cumin, stir and rub steak with this mix.
2. Season steak with salt and pepper, rub again with the oil, position it in the air fryer and for 20 minutes boil at 400 degrees F, flipping them halfway.
3. Move the steak to a cutting board, slice and serve with a side salad.
4. Enjoy!

PER SERVING

Calories:320 | Fat:8g |Carbohydrates: 22g | Protein: 21g

Pork Tenderloin with Mustard Glazed

Prep time: 10 minutes | Cook time: 18 minutes | Serves 4

- Yellow mustard: ¼ cup
- One pork tenderloin
- Salt: ¼ tsp
- Freshly ground black pepper: ⅛ tsp
- Minced garlic: 1 Tbsp.
- Dried rosemary: 1 tsp
- Italian seasoning: 1 tsp

1. Cut the top of pork tenderloin. Add minced garlic in the cuts, and season with salt and pepper.
2. In a bowl, add mustard, rosemary, and Italian seasoning mix until combined. Rub this mustard mix all over pork.
3. Let it marinate in the refrigerator for two hours.
4. Put pork tenderloin in the air fryer basket. Cook for 18 minutes at 400°F. with an instant-read thermometer internal temperature of pork should be 145°F.
5. Take out from the air fryer and serve.

PER SERVING

Calories: 389.5 | Protein: 59.6g | Carbs: 10.5g | Fat: 10.4g

Meatballs In Tomato Sauce

Prep time: 10 minutes | Cook time: 12 minutes | Serves 3–4

- 1 egg
- ¾ lb. lean ground beef
- 1 onion, chopped
- 3 tbsp. breadcrumbs
- ½ tbsp. fresh thyme leaves, chopped
- ½ cup tomato sauce
- 1 tbsp. parsley, chopped
- Pinch salt
- Pinch pepper, to taste

1. Preheat the Air Fryer to 390°F
2. Place all ingredients in a bowl. Mix until well-combined. Divide mixture into 12 balls. Place them in the cooking basket. Cook meatballs for 8 minutes.
3. Put the cooked meatballs in an oven dish. Pour the tomato sauce on top. Put the oven dish inside the cooking basket of the Air Fryer. Cook for 5 minutes at 330°F.

PER SERVING

Calorie: 128.4 | Carbs: 14.7g | Fat: 17.1g | Protein: 18.2g | Fiber: 1.2g

Chinese Steak and Broccoli

Prep time: 45 minutes | Cook time:12 minutes |Serves 4

- 3/4-pound round steak, cut into strips
- 1-pound broccoli florets
- 1/3 cup oyster sauce
- 2 teaspoons sesame oil
- 1 teaspoon soy sauce
- 1 teaspoon sugar
- 1/3 cup sherry
- 1 tablespoon olive oil
- 1 garlic clove, minced

1. In a bowl, mix sesame oil with oyster sauce, soy sauce, sherry, and sugar, stir well.
2. Add beef, toss, and leave aside for 30 minutes.
3. Transfer beef to a pan that fits your air fryer, add broccoli, garlic, and oil, toss everything.
4. Cook at 380 degrees F for 12 minutes.
5. Divide among plates and serve.
6. Enjoy!

PER SERVING

Calories:330 | Fat:12g |Carbohydrates: 23g | Protein: 23g

Provencal Pork
Prep time: 10 minutes | Cook time:15 minutes |Serves 2

- 1 red onion, sliced
- 1 yellow bell pepper, cut into strips
- 1 green bell pepper, cut into strips
- Salt and black pepper to the taste
- 2 teaspoons Provencal herbs
- 1/2 tablespoon mustard
- 1 tablespoon olive oil
- 7 ounces pork tenderloin

1. Using a baking dish in the air fryer, mix yellow bell pepper with green bell pepper, onion, salt, pepper, Provencal herbs, and half of the oil and toss well.
2. Season pork with salt, pepper, mustard, and the rest of the oil, toss well and add to veggies.
3. Introduce everything in your air fryer, cook at 370 degrees F for 15 minutes.
4. Divide among plates and serve.
5. Enjoy!

PER SERVING

Calories:300 | Fat:8g |Carbohydrates: 21g | Protein: 23g

Flavorful Meatballs
Prep time: 15 minutes | Cook time: 25 minutes | Serves 6

- 200 g ground beef
- 200 g ground chicken
- 100 g ground pork
- 30 g minced garlic
- 1 potato
- 1 egg
- 1 tsp. basil
- 1 tsp. cayenne pepper
- 1 tsp. white pepper
- 2 tsp. olive oil

1. Combine ground beef, chicken meat, and pork in the mixing bowl and stir it gently.
2. Sprinkle it with basil, cayenne pepper, and white pepper.
3. Add minced garlic and egg. Stir the mixture gently. You should get a fluffy mass.
4. Peel the potato and grate it. Add grated potato to the mixture and stir it again.
5. Preheat the air fryer oven to 375°F. Take a tray and spray it with olive oil.
6. Make the balls from the meat mass and put them on the tray. Lay the tray in the oven and cook it for 25 minutes.

PER SERVING

Calories: 203.5 | Protein: 26.5g | Fat: 7.1g | Carbs: 6.5g

Meatballs In Spicy Tomato Sauce
Prep time: 5 minutes | Cook time: 15 minutes | Serves 4

- 3 green onions, minced
- 1 garlic clove, minced
- 1 egg yolk
- ¼-cup saltine cracker crumbs
- Pinch salt
- Freshly ground black pepper
- 1 pound 95 percent lean ground beef
- Olive oil for misting
- 1¼ cups pasta sauce
- 2 tablespoons Dijon mustard

1. In a large bowl, combine the green onions, garlic, egg yolk, cracker crumbs, salt, and pepper, and mix well.
2. Add the ground beef and mix thoroughly with the hands until combined. Form into 1½-inch meatballs. Mist the meatballs with olive oil and put into the basket of the air fryer.
3. Bake for 8 to 11 minutes or until the meatballs are 165°F. Remove the meatballs from the basket and place in a 6-inch metal bowl. Top with the pasta sauce and Dijon mustard and mix gently.
4. Bake for 4 minutes until the sauce is hot.

PER SERVING

Calories: 359.5 | Fat: 11.3g | Carbs: 23.5g | Fiber: 3g | Protein: 39.5g

Air Fryer Pork Satay
Prep time: 15 minutes | Cook time: 10 minutes | Serves 4

- 1 (1 lb./454 g.) pork tenderloin, cut into 1 1/2-inch cubes
- 1/4 cup onion, minced
- 2 garlic cloves, minced
- 1 jalapeño pepper, minced
- 2 tbsp. lime juice, freshly squeezed
- 2 tbsp. coconut milk
- 2 tbsp. unsalted peanut butter
- 2 tsp. curry powder

1. In a medium bowl, mix the pork, lime juice, garlic, onion, jalapeño, peanut butter, coconut milk, and curry powder until well combined. Let position for 10 minutes at room temperature.
2. Remove the pork from the marinade but reserve the marinade.
3. Thread the pork onto 8 skewers. Air fry at 380°F for 10 minutes, brushing once with the reserved marinade until the pork reaches at least 145°F on a meat thermometer.
4. Discard any remaining marinade and serve immediately.

PER SERVING

Calories: 194.5 | Fats: 24.5g | Protein: 7.6g | Carbs: 1g, Fibers: 1g | Sugars: 2.5g

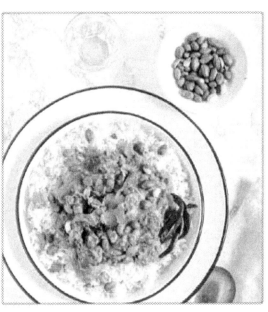

Paprika Pulled Pork

Prep time: 15 minutes | Cook time: 25 minutes | Serves 4

- 1 tbsp. chili flakes
- 1 tsp. ground black pepper
- ½ tsp. paprika
- 1 tsp. cayenne pepper
- ⅓ cup cream
- 1 tsp. kosher salt
- 1-lb. pork tenderloin
- 1 tsp. ground thyme
- 4 cup chicken stock
- 1 tsp. butter

1. Pour the chicken stock into the air fryer basket tray.
2. Add the pork steak and sprinkle the mixture with chili flakes, paprika, cayenne pepper, ground black pepper, and salt. Preheat the air fryer to 370°F and cook the meat for 20 minutes.
3. Strain the liquid and shred the meat with 2 forks.
4. Then add the butter and cream and mix it.
5. Cook the pulled pork for 4 minutes more at 360°F. When the pulled pork is cooked allow to rest briefly.

PER SERVING

Calories: 197.5 | Fat: 6.2g | Fiber: 0.5g | Carbs: 2.1g | Protein: 31.2

Pork Almond Bites

Prep time: 10 minutes | Cook time: 14 minutes | Serves 6

- 1-lb. pork tenderloin
- 2 eggs
- 1 tsp. butter
- ¼ cup almond flour
- 1 tsp. kosher salt
- 1 tsp. paprika
- 1 tsp. ground coriander
- ½ tsp. lemon zest

1. Chop the pork tenderloin into the large cubes.
2. Sprinkle the pork cubes with ground coriander, paprika, kosher salt, and lemon zest.
3. Mix the meat gently. Crack the egg into a bowl and whisk it. Coat the meat cubes with the egg mixture and then the almond flour.
4. Preheat the air fryer to 365°F.
5. Put the butter in the air fryer basket tray and then place the pork bites inside. Cook for 14 minutes.
6. Turn the pork bites over after 7 minutes of cooking.
7. When the pork bites are cooked – serve them hot.

PER SERVING

Calories: 141.5 | Fat: 5.1g | Fiber: 0.3g | Carbs: 0.5g | Protein: 22.2

Chapter 7
Fish and Seafood

Asian Sesame Cod

Prep time: 5 minutes | Cook time: 10 minutes | Serves 1

- 1 tablespoon reduced-sodium soy sauce
- 2 teaspoons honey
- 1 teaspoon sesame seeds
- 6 ounces (170 g) cod fillet

1. In a lesser bowl, syndicate the soy sauce and honey.
2. Sprig the air fryer basket with nonstick cooking spray, then place the fish in the basket, brush with the soy mixture, and sprinkle with sesame seeds. Roast at 360°F for 10 minutes or until opaque.
3. Remove the fryer's fish and allow cooling on a wire rack for 5 minutes before serving.

PER SERVING

Calories: 140.4 | Fat: 1g | Protein: 26.5g | Carbs: 6.5g | Fiber: 1g, Sugar: 6g

Scallops with Tomato Sauce

Prep time: 5 minutes | Cook time: 10 minutes | Serves 2

- Sea scallops eight jumbo
- Tomato Paste: 1 tbsp.
- Chopped fresh basil one tablespoon
- 3/4 cup of low-fat Whipping Cream
- Kosher salt half teaspoon
- Ground Freshly black pepper half teaspoon
- Minced garlic 1 teaspoon
- Frozen Spinach, thawed half cup
- Oil Spray

1. Take a seven-inch pan (heatproof) and add spinach in a single layer at the bottom
2. Rub olive oil on both sides of scallops, season with kosher salt and pepper.
3. On top of the spinach, place the seasoned scallops
4. Put the pan in the air fryer and cook for ten minutes at 350°F, until scallops are cooked completely, and internal temperature reaches 135°F. Serve immediately.

PER SERVING

Calories: 258.5 | Protein: 18.5g | Carbs: 5.4g | Fat: 12.5g

Paprika Cod and Endives

Prep time:5 minutes |Cook time: 20 minutes |Serves 4

- 2 endives, shredded
- 2 tablespoons olive oil
- Salt and back pepper to the taste
- 4 salmon fillets, boneless
- ½ teaspoon sweet paprika

1. In a pan that fits the air fryer, combine the fish with the rest of the ingredients, toss, introduce in the fryer and cook at 350 degrees F for 20 minutes, flipping the fish halfway.
2. Divide between plates and serve right away.

Per Serving
Calories 243| Fat 13| Fiber 3| Carbs 6| Protein 14

Turmeric Salmon

Prep time:10 minutes |Cook time: 7 minutes |Serves 2

- 8 oz salmon fillet
- 2 tablespoons coconut flakes
- 1 tablespoon coconut cream
- ½ teaspoon salt
- ½ teaspoon ground turmeric
- ½ teaspoon onion powder
- 1 teaspoon nut oil

1. Cut the salmon fillet into halves and sprinkle with salt, ground turmeric, and onion powder.
2. After this, dip the fish fillets in the coconut cream and coat in the coconut flakes.
3. Sprinkle the salmon fillets with nut oil.
4. Preheat the air fryer to 380F.
5. Arrange the salmon fillets in the air fryer basket and cook for 7 minutes.

PER SERVING

Calories 209| Fat 12.8| Fiber 0.8| Carbs 0.2| Protein 22.4

Fish Finger Sandwich

Prep time: 10 minutes | Cook time: 15 minutes | Serves 3

- Greek yogurt: 1 tbsp.
- Cod fillets: 4, without skin
- Flour: 2 tbsp.
- Whole-wheat breadcrumbs: 5 tbsp.
- Kosher salt and pepper to taste
- Capers: 10–12
- Frozen peas: 3/4 cup
- Lemon juice

1. Let the air fryer preheat.
2. Sprinkle kosher salt and pepper on the cod fillets, and coat in flour, then in breadcrumbs.
3. Spray the fryer basket with oil. Put the cod fillets in the basket. Cook for 15 minutes at 400° F.
4. Meanwhile, cook the peas in boiling water for a few minutes. Take out from the water and blend with Greek yogurt, lemon juice, and capers until well combined.
5. On a bun, add cooked fish with pea puree. Add lettuce and tomato.

PER SERVING

Calories: 239.5 | Protein: 20.5g | Carbs: 6.5g | Fat: 11.5g

Salmon and Lime Sauce

Prep time:5 minutes |Cook time: 20 minutes |Serves 4

- 4 salmon fillets, boneless
- ¼ cup coconut cream
- 1 teaspoon lime zest, grated
- 1/3 cup heavy cream
- ¼ cup lime juice
- ½ cup coconut, shredded Apinch of salt and black pepper

1. In a bowl, mix all the ingredients except the salmon and whisk.
2. Arrange the fish in a pan that fits your air fryer, drizzle the coconut sauce all over, put the pan in the machine and cook at 360 degrees F for 20 minutes.
3. Divide between plates and serve.

PER SERVING

Calories 227| Fat 12| Fiber 2| Carbs 4| Protein 9

Baked Salmon Patties

Prep time: 10 minutes | Cook time: 20 minutes | Serves 4

- 2 eggs, lightly beaten
- 12 oz. can salmon, skinless, boneless, and drained
- ½ cup almond flour
- ½ tsp. pepper
- 1 tbsp. Dijon mustard
- 1 tsp. garlic powder
- 2 tbsp. fresh parsley, chopped
- ½ cup celery, diced
- ½ cup bell pepper, diced
- ½ cup onion, diced

1. Add salmon and remaining ingredients into the mixing bowl and mix until well combined.
2. Make 8 equal shapes of patties from the mixture.
3. Place the cooking tray in the air fryer basket. Line air fryer basket with parchment paper.
4. Select Bake mode. Set time to 20 minutes and temperature 400°F then press START.
5. The air fryer display will prompt you to ADD FOOD once the temperature is reached then place patties in the air fryer basket. Turn patties halfway through. Serve and enjoy.

PER SERVING

Calories: 181.7 | Fat: 6.1g | Carbs: 4.3g, Sugar 2g, Protein 23.2g

Crispy Herbed Salmon

Prep time: 5 minutes | Cook time:10 minutes |Serves 4

- 4 (6-ounce) skinless salmon fillets
- 3 tablespoons honey mustard
- 1/2 teaspoon dried thyme
- 1/2 teaspoon dried basil
- 1/4 cup panko breadcrumbs
- 1/3 cup crushed potato chips
- 2 tablespoons olive oil

1. Place the salmon on a plate. Get a bowl, combine the mustard, thyme, and basil, and spread evenly over the salmon.
2. In another small bowl, combine the breadcrumbs and potato chips and mix well. Drizzle in the olive oil and mix until combined.
3. Place the salmon in the air fryer basket and gently but firmly press the bread crumb mixture onto the top of each fillet.
4. Cook until the salmon reaches at least 145F on a meat thermometer, and the topping is browned and crisp.

PER SERVING

Calories:373 | Fat:21g |Carbohydrates: 13g | Protein: 34g

Catfish Bites

Prep time:10 minutes |Cook time: 10 minutes |Serves 4

- ¼ cup coconut flakes
- 3 tablespoons coconut flour
- 1 teaspoon salt
- 3 eggs, beaten
- 10 oz catfish fillet
- Cooking spray

1. Cut the catfish fillet on the small pieces (nuggets) and sprinkle with salt.
2. After this, dip the catfish pieces in the egg and coat in the coconut flour.
3. Then dip the fish pieces in the egg again and coat in the coconut flakes.
4. Preheat the air fryer to 385F.
5. Place the catfish nuggets in the air fryer basket and cook them for 6 minutes.
6. Then flip the nuggets on another side and cook them for 4 minutes more.

PER SERVING

Calories 187| Fat 11.3| Fiber 2.7| Carbs 4.4| Protein 16.5

Tuna Skewers

Prep time:5 minutes |Cook time: 12 minutes |Serves 4

- 1 pound tuna steaks, boneless and cubed
- 1 chili pepper, minced
- 4 green onions, chopped
- 2 tablespoons lime juice Adrizzle of olive oil
- Salt and black pepper to the taste

1. In a bowl mix all the ingredients and toss them.
2. Thread the tuna cubes on skewers, arrange them in your air fryer's basket and cook at 370 degrees F for 12 minutes.
3. Divide between plates and serve with a side salad.

PER SERVING

Calories 226| Fat 12| Fiber 2| Carbs 4| Protein 15

Moist & Juicy Baked Cod

Prep time: 10 minutes | Cook time: 10 minutes | Serves 2

- 1 lb. cod fillets
- 1 ½ tbsp. olive oil
- 3 dashes cayenne pepper
- 1 tbsp. lemon juice
- ¼ tsp. salt

1. In a small bowl, mix together olive oil, cayenne pepper, lemon juice, and salt.
2. Brush fish fillets with oil mixture.
3. Place the cooking tray in the air fryer basket. Line air fryer basket with parchment paper.
4. Select Bake mode. Set time to 10 minutes and temperature 400°F then press START.

5. The air fryer display will prompt you to ADD FOOD once the temperature is reached then place fish fillets in the air fryer basket. Serve and enjoy.

PER SERVING

Calories: 274.8 | Fat: 12.1g | Carbs: 0.4g, Sugar 0.2g, Protein 40.9g

Mustard Cod

Prep time:10 minutes |Cook time: 14 minutes |Serves 4

- 1 cup parmesan, grated
- 4 cod fillets, boneless
- Salt and black pepper to the taste
- 1 tablespoon mustard

1. In a bowl, mix the parmesan with salt, pepper and the mustard and stir.
2. Spread this over the cod, arrange the fish in the air fryer's basket and cook at 370 degrees F for 7 minutes on each side.
3. Divide between plates and serve with a side salad.

PER SERVING

Calories 270| Fat 14| Fiber 3| Carbs 5| Protein 12

Butter Mussels

Prep time:10 minutes |Cook time: 2 minutes |Serves5

- 2-pounds mussels
- 1 shallot, chopped
- 1 tablespoon minced garlic
- 1 tablespoon butter, melted
- 1 teaspoon sunflower oil
- 1 teaspoon salt
- 1 tablespoon fresh parsley, chopped
- ½ teaspoon chili flakes

1. Clean and wash mussels and put them in the big bowl.
2. Add shallot, minced garlic, butter, sunflower oil, salt, and chili flakes.
3. Shake the mussels well.
4. Preheat the air fryer to 390F.
5. Put the mussels in the air fryer basket and cook for 2 minutes.
6. Then transfer the cooked meal in the serving bowl and top it with chopped fresh parsley.

PER SERVING

Calories 192| Fat 7.3| Fiber 0.1| Carbs 8.3| Protein 21.9

Shrimp Tacos
Prep time: 5 minutes | Cook time: 8 minutes | Serves 4

- 1 lb peeled, deveined shrimp
- 1/2 teaspoon chili powder
- 1/4 teaspoon cumin
- pinch salt
- 4 flour tortillas
- sliced avocado
- cilantro
- lime
- crumbled cotija cheese
- green shredded cabbage
- pinch pepper
- 1/4 teaspoon onion powder
- 1/2 teaspoon garlic powder
- 2 tablespoons oil

1. In a bowl, toss shrimp with oil, chili powder, garlic powder, cumin, onion powder, salt, and pepper. Transfer to a greased air fryer basket.
2. Air fry at 400°F for 5-6 minutes.
3. Assemble tacos with shrimp and cabbage in tortillas; place them in the air fryer basket and air fry at 400°F for 1 minute to warm up the tortillas.
4. Remove tacos from the basket and add toppings. Serve immediately.

PER SERVING

Calories: 454Kcal | Fat: 20g | Carbs: 37g | Protein: 32g | Sugar: 1g | Sodium: 1375mg

Seafood Tacos
Prep time: 15 minutes | Cook time:10 minutes |Serves 2

- 1-pound white fish fillets, such as snapper
- 1 tablespoon olive oil
- 3 tablespoons lemon juice, divided
- 11/2 cups chopped red cabbage
- 1/2 cup salsa
- 1/3 cup sour cream
- 6 soft flour tortillas
- 2 avocados, peeled and chopped

1. Brush the fish with olive oil and sprinkle with 1 tablespoon of lemon juice.
2. Place in the air fryer basket and air-fry for 9 to 12 minutes or until the fish flakes when tested with a fork.
3. Meanwhile, combine the remaining 2 tablespoons of lemon juice, cabbage, salsa, and sour cream in a medium bowl.
4. When the fish is cooked, remove it from the air fryer basket and break it into large pieces.
5. Let everyone assemble their taco combining the fish, tortillas, cabbage mixture, and avocados.

PER SERVING

Calories:491 | Fat:29g |Carbohydrates: 29g | Protein: 31g

Tuna Cakes
Prep time: 10 minutes | Cook time: 12 minutes | Serves 12

- 2 - 12 oz. cans of chunk tuna in water
- 1/2 cup seasoned breadcrumbs
- 2 tablespoon lemon juice
- 1/2 teaspoon salt
- 2 eggs
- 4 tablespoon mayo
- 1/2 diced white onion
- 1/2 teaspoon black pepper

1. Mix the ingredients in a large bowl.
2. Form the mixture into patties and place them into a cooking basket in your air fryer.
3. Cook at 375 °F for 12 minutes, flipping at half-time.
4. Remove and serve immediately.

PER SERVING

Calories: 83Kcal | Fat: 0g | Carbs: 4g | Protein: 5g | Sugar: 1g | Sodium: 260mg

Coconut Shrimp

Prep time: 10 minutes | Cook time: 12 minutes | Serves 4

- 1 pound shrimp raw
- ½ teaspoon salt
- 2 large eggs
- ¼ cup breadcrumbs
- sweet chili sauce for serving
- ¼ cup all-purpose flour
- ¼ teaspoon black pepper
- ¾ cup unsweetened shredded coconut
- cooking spray

1. To make coconut shrimp, preheat the air fryer to 360°F.
2. Spray the basket with cooking spray.
3. To make the batter, whisk together flour, salt, and pepper in one shallow bowl. Whisk together eggs and shredded coconut in another shallow bowl.
4. Combine panko breadcrumbs with salt-and-pepper seasoning in a third shallow bowl.
5. Dip shrimp into flour mixture, shaking off excess; then dredge into eggs; finally, press into coconut mixture to coat evenly.
6. Place on top of shrimp so they are not touching; spray top with oil or cooking spray.
7. Cook for 10-12 minutes, flipping halfway through until golden brown on both sides

PER SERVING

Calories: 304Kcal | Fat: 15g | Carbs: 13g | Protein: 28g | Sugar: 2g | Sodium: 1237mg

Asian Steamed Tuna

Prep time: 10 minutes | Cook time:10 minutes |Serves 4

- 4 small tuna steaks
- 2 tablespoons low-sodium soy sauce
- 2 teaspoons sesame oil
- 2 teaspoons rice wine vinegar
- 1 teaspoon grated fresh ginger
- 1/8 teaspoon pepper
- 1 stalk lemongrass, bent in half
- 3 tablespoons lemon juice

1. Place the tuna steaks on a plate.
2. Put the soy sauce, sesame oil, rice wine vinegar, ginger, and mix well in a small bowl.
3. Pour this mixture over the tuna and marinate for 10 minutes.
4. Rub the soy sauce mixture gently into both sides of the tuna. Sprinkle with pepper.
5. Place the lemongrass on the air fryer basket and top with the steaks. Put the lemon juice and 1 tablespoon water in the pan below the basket.
6. Cook fish for 10 minutes or until the tuna registers at least 145°F. Discard the lemongrass and serve the tuna.
7. Air Fryer tip: Keep an eye on the liquid in the pan below the air fryer basket when this recipe is cooking. The tuna will give off liquid as it cooks, and you don't want the pan to overflow.

PER SERVING

Calories:292 | Fat:14g |Carbohydrates: 1g | Protein: 38g

Salmon and Garlic Sauce

Prep time:5 minutes |Cook time: 15 minutes |Serves 4

- 3 tablespoons parsley, chopped
- 4 salmon fillets, boneless
- ¼ cup ghee, melted
- 2 garlic cloves, minced
- 4 shallots, chopped
- Salt and black pepper to the taste

1. Heat up a pan that fits the air fryer with the ghee over medium-high heat, add the garlic, shallots, salt, pepper and the parsley, stir and cook for 5 minutes.
2. Add the salmon fillets, toss gently, introduce the pan in the air fryer and cook at 380 degrees F for 15 minutes.
3. Divide between plates and serve.

PER SERVING

Calories 270| Fat 12| Fiber 2| Carbs 4| Protein 17

Chapter 8
Vegetables and Side Dishes

Cheese Stuffed Mushrooms

Prep time: 15 minutes | Cook time: 7 minutes | Serves 3

- 9 large button mushrooms, stems removed
- 1 tbsp. olive oil
- Salt and ground black pepper, to taste
- 1/2 tsp. rosemary, dried
- 6 tbsp. Swiss cheese, shredded
- 6 tbsp. Romano cheese, shredded
- 6 tbsp. cream cheese
- 1 tsp. soy sauce
- 1 tsp. garlic, minced
- 3 tbsp. green onion, minced

1. Brush the mushroom caps with olive oil; sprinkle with salt, pepper, and rosemary.
2. In a mixing bowl, thoroughly combine the remaining ingredients, mix them well, and divide the filling mixture among the mushroom caps. Cook in the preheated air fryer at 390°F for 7 minutes.
3. Let the mushrooms cool slightly before serving.

PER SERVING

Calories: 344.5 | Fat: 27.5g | Carbs: 10.6g | Protein: 14.8g | Sugars: 7.5g

Fried Pickles

Prep time: 20 minutes | Cook time: 10 minutes | Serves 2

- 1 egg, whisked
- 2 tablespoons of buttermilk
- 1/2 cup of fresh breadcrumbs
- 1/4 cup of Romano cheese, grated
- 1/2 teaspoon of onion powder
- 1/2 teaspoon of garlic powder
- 1½ cups of dill pickle chips, pressed dry with kitchen towels

MAYO SAUCE:

- 1/4 cup of mayonnaise
- 1/2 tablespoon of mustard
- 1/2 teaspoon of molasses
- 1 tablespoon of ketchup
- 1/4 teaspoon of ground black pepper

1. In a shallow bowl, whisk the egg with buttermilk.
2. In another bowl, mix the onion powder, cheese, breadcrumbs, and garlic powder.
3. Dip the pickle chips in the egg mixture, then, dredge with the mixture.
4. Cook in the preheated Air Fryer at 400°F for 5 minutes; shake the basket and cook for 5 minutes more.
5. Meanwhile, mix all the sauce ingredients until well combined. Serve the fried pickles with the mayo sauce for dipping.

PER SERVING

Calories: 341.5 | Fat: 28.1g | Carbs: 12.2g | Protein: 9.8g | Sugars: 4.2g

Air-Fryer Asparags

Prep time: 20 minutes | Cook time: 4 minutes | Serves 2

- ½ pound fresh asparagus, trimmed
- 1/8 cup mayonnaise
- 2 teaspoons olive oil
- lemon wedges
- 1 teaspoon grated lemon zest
- 1 tablespoon shredded parmesan cheese
- 1/8 teaspoon seasoned salt
- ½ garlic clove, minced
- ¼ teaspoon pepper

1. Preheat the air fryer to 350°F.
2. To cook asparagus in air fryer, preheat the air fryer to 375°F.
3. Add asparagus and toss to coat. Working in batches, place asparagus on a greased tray in the air-fryer basket.
4. Cook until tender and lightly browned, 4–6 minutes. Now transfer this to a platter and sprinkle with some Parmesan cheese. If desired, serve with lemon wedges.

PER SERVING

Calories: 156| Fat: 15g | Carbs: 3g | Protein: 2g | Sugar: 1g | Sodium: 214mg

Cauliflower Tater Tots

Prep time: 15 minutes | Cook time:16 minutes |Serves 12

- 1pound (454 g) cauliflower, steamed and chopped
- 1/2 cup Nutritional yeast
- 1 tablespoon oats
- 1 tablespoon desiccated coconuts
- 3 tablespoons flaxseed meal
- 3 tablespoons water
- 1 onion, chopped
- 1 teaspoon minced garlic
- 1 teaspoon chopped parsley
- 1 teaspoon chopped oregano
- 1 teaspoon chopped chives
- Salt and ground black pepper, to taste
- 1/2 cup breadcrumbs

1. Preheat the air fryer oven to 390F (199C).
2. Drain any excess water out of the cauliflower by wringing it with a paper towel.
3. Mix the cauliflower with the remaining ingredients, save the breadcrumbs. Using the hands, shape the mixture into several small balls.
4. Coat the balls in the breadcrumbs and transfer to the air fryer
5. Change temperature to 400 degrees F and air fry for an additional 10 minutes.
6. Serve immediately.

PER SERVING

Calories:147 | Fat:6g |Carbohydrates: 20g | Protein: 3g

Herb and Lemon Cauliflower
Prep time: 20 minutes | Cook time: 5 minutes | Serves 2

- 1 tablespoon lemon juice
- 2 tablespoons olive oil, divided
- 1/8 teaspoon crushed red pepper flakes
- 1/8 cup minced fresh parsley
- ½ medium head cauliflower, cut into florets
- ½ tablespoon minced fresh rosemary
- 1/4 teaspoon salt
- ½ tablespoon minced fresh thyme
- ½ teaspoon grated lemon zest

1. Take a large bowl and add the cauliflower florets to the bowl. Drizzle it with olive oil to make sure the cauliflower is coated well.
2. Arrange the cauliflower on the tray in a Pre-heated air fryer basket. Place them in a single layer so that they can cook evenly.
3. Cook until they are tender and edges are browned, 8-10 minutes, stirring halfway through.
4. In a small bowl, combine the remaining ingredients and toss with the remaining 2 tablespoons olive oil.
5. Dish the cauliflower in a large mixing bowl; drizzle with the herb mixture and toss to combine.

PER SERVING

Calories: 161| Fat: 14g | Carbs: 8g | Protein: 3g | Sugar: 3g | Sodium: 342mg

Paprika Cauliflower Soup
Prep time: 10 minutes | Cook time:35 minutes |Serves 4

- 360 g bell peppers, red or green
- 320 g cauliflower
- 23 g olive oil
- 18 g spring onion
- 4 g garlic
- 90 g feta
- 90 ml pastry cream
- 540 ml chicken broth-3 cups
- 1/2 tsp paprika spice seasoning
- 1/2 tsp thyme
- 1/2 tsp red pepper flakes
- salt
- pepper

1. Set the air fryer to grill and preheat to 200° C. Cut the peppers in half and core them.
2. Then moisten with olive oil inside and outside.
3. Put the peppers on the baking tray (use parchment paper) and grill for 10-15 minutes.
4. While the peppers are cooking, cut the cauliflower into florets.
5. Remove the ready-grilled peppers from the air fryer and place in zip-closed freezer bags or a container with a lid. Now place the cauliflower florets on the baking sheet.
6. Mix 1 tbsp olive oil with salt and pepper. Use it to coat the cauliflower.
7. Put the plate in the air fryer and cook the cauliflower for 30 to 35 minutes at 200° C with circulating air (do not forget to switch from "grilling" to "convection").
8. Remove the skin from the peppers.
9. Dice the spring onions. Heat 2 tablespoon of olive oil in the pot and sauté the onions.
10. Once the spring onions are seared, add the spices. Mix everything well and let the spices release their aroma.
11. Now add the peppers. Let them fry for a moment. Then add the chicken broth, red pepper, and cauliflower.
12. Simmer for another 10-20 minutes at low temperature.
13. .Pour the pastry cream into it. Take the soup from the hob and purée with a blender for about 2 minutes.
14. Season to taste. Before serving, dice the feta cheese, spread on top and garnish with thyme and spring onions.

PER SERVING

Calories:68 | Fat:4g |Carbohydrates: 8g | Protein: 1g

Family Vegetable Gratin
Prep time: 35 minutes | Cook time: 30 minutes | Serves 4

- 1-pound Chinese cabbage, roughly chopped
- 2 bell peppers, seeded and sliced
- 1 jalapeno pepper, seeded and sliced
- 1 onion, thickly sliced
- 2 garlic cloves, sliced
- 1/2 stick butter
- 4 tablespoons all-purpose flour
- 1 cup milk
- 1 cup cream cheese
- Sea salt and freshly ground black pepper, to taste
- 1/2 teaspoon cayenne pepper
- 1 cup Monterey Jack cheese, shredded

1. Heat a pan of salted water and bring to a boil. Boil the Chinese cabbage for 2 to 3 minutes. Transfer to cold water to stop the cooking process.
2. Place the cabbage in a lightly greased casserole dish. Add the onion, peppers, and garlic.
3. Next, melt the butter in a saucepan over moderate heat. Gradually add the flour and cook for 2 minutes to form a paste.
4. Slowly pour in the milk, stirring until a thick sauce form. Add the cream cheese.
5. Season with the black pepper, salt, and cayenne pepper. Add the mixture to the casserole dish.
6. Top with the shredded Monterey Jack cheese and bake in the preheated Air Fryer at 390 degrees F for 25 minutes.

Potato with Creamy Cheese
Prep time: 5 minutes | Cook time:15 minutes |Serves 2

- 2 medium potatoes
- 1 teaspoon butter
- 3 tablespoons sour cream
- 1 teaspoon chives
- 1 1/2 tablespoons grated Parmesan cheese

1. Preheat the air fryer oven to 350 degrees F.
2. Stick the potatoes with a fork and boil them in water until they are cooked. Move to the air fryer basket and cook for 15 minutes.
3. In the meantime, combine the sour cream, cheese, and chives in bowl.
4. Cut the potatoes halfway to open them up and fill with the butter and sour cream mixture.
5. Serve immediately.

PER SERVING

Calories:184 | Fat:2g |Carbohydrates: 38g | Protein: 5g

Air Fryer Buffalo Cauliflower
Prep time: 5 minutes | Cook time: 15 minutes | Serves 4

- Homemade buffalo sauce: 1/2 cup
- One head of cauliflower, cut bite-size pieces
- Butter melted: 1 tablespoon
- Olive oil
- Kosher salt & pepper, to taste

1. Spray cooking oil on the air fryer basket.
2. In a bowl, add melted butter, buffalo sauce, pepper, and salt. Mix well.
3. Put the cauliflower bits in the air fryer and spray the olive oil over it. Let it cook at 400 F for 7 minutes.
4. Remove the cauliflower from the air fryer and add it to the sauce. Coat the cauliflower well.
5. Put the sauce coated cauliflower back into the air fryer.
6. Cook at 400 F, for 7-8 minutes. Take out from the air fryer and serve with dipping sauce.

PER SERVING

Calories: 100.8 | Carbs: 3.7g | Protein: 3.5g | Fat: 6.5g

Hot Chili Soup

Prep time: 10 minutes | Cook time:20 minutes |Serves 4

- 2 tbsp olive oil
- 2 pieces of chili peppers fresh
- 360 ml chicken broth
- 360 ml water
- 1/2 tsp Ground cumin
- 32 g tomato paste
- 350 g chicken meat
- 30 g butter
- 1 avocado
- 60 g cream cheese
- 15 ml lime juice
- salt
- pepper

1. Core chili peppers and cut into small pieces.
2. Cut the chicken into small pieces.
3. Coat an air fryer with olive oil and sauté the meat and set aside.
4. Heat 2 tbsp of olive oil in air fryer, add the coriander seeds and wait until they develop their aroma.
5. Do all pieces of chili peppers.
6. Add chicken stock and water into the pot and let it boil.
7. Season with cumin, salt, and pepper.
8. Bring the soup to a boil briefly.
9. Then stir in the tomato paste and butter.
10. Now simmer the soup for another 5 to 10 minutes. Add lime juice.
11. Put 1/4 of the meat in a soup plate (or bowl), fill with soup and refine with 1 spoon of cream cheese. Garnish with coriander.
12. If necessary, season with salt and pepper.
13. Slice the avocado and place 1/4 of each in a soup plate.

PER SERVING

Calories:199 | Fat:2g |Carbohydrates: 24g | Protein: 21g

Okra with Smoked Paprika

Prep time: 10 minutes | Cook time: 10 minutes | Serves 2

- 1/8 teaspoon salt
- 1/2 pound fresh okra pods
- 1/8 teaspoon pepper
- ½ tablespoon olive oil
- 1/8 teaspoon garlic powder
- ½ tablespoon lemon juice
- 1/4 teaspoon smoked paprika

1. Preheat the air fryer to 375°F. Add all the ingredients into a bowl and mix them until they are combined, then spread evenly onto a greased tray.
2. Put the okra in the air fryer basket and cook until tender and lightly browned, 15-20 minutes, stirring occasionally.

PER SERVING

Calories: 57Kcal | Fat: 4g | Carbs: 6g | Protein: 2g | Sugar: 3g | Sodium: 155mg

Roasted Broccoli with Sesame Seeds

Prep time: 15 minutes | Cook time: 10 minutes | Serves 2

- 1 pound broccoli florets
- 2 tablespoons of sesame oil
- 1/2 teaspoon of shallot powder
- 1/2 teaspoon of porcini powder
- 1 teaspoon of garlic powder
- Salt and pepper to taste
- 1/2 teaspoon of cumin powder
- 1/4 teaspoon of paprika
- 2 tablespoons of sesame seeds

1. Start by warming the Air Fryer to 400°F.
2. Blanch the broccoli in salted boiling water until al dente, about 4 minutes. Drain well and transfer to the lightly greased Air Fryer basket.
3. Add the shallot powder, porcini powder, sesame oil, cumin powder, garlic powder, salt, black pepper, paprika, and sesame seeds. Cook for 6 minutes, tossing them over halfway through the Cooking Time.

PER SERVING

Calories: 266.5 | Fat: 19.1g | Carbs: 19.6g | Protein: 9.6g | Sugars: 4.6g

Vegetable Braise

Prep time: 25 minutes | Cook time: 20 minutes | Serves 2

- 4 potatoes, peeled and cut into 1-inch pieces
- 1 celery root, peeled and cut into 1-inch pieces
- 1 cup winter squash
- 2 tablespoons unsalted butter, melted
- 1/2 cup chicken broth
- 1/4 cup tomato sauce
- 1 teaspoon parsley
- 1 teaspoon rosemary
- 1 teaspoon thyme

1. Start by preheating your Air Fryer to 370 degrees F.
2. Add all ingredients in a lightly greased casserole dish. Stir to combine well.
3. Bake in the Air Fryer for 10 minutes. Stir the vegetables with a large spoon and increase the temperature to 400 degrees F; cook for 10 minutes more.
4. Serve in individual bowls with a few drizzles of lemon juice.

PER SERVING

Calories: 357.5 | Fat: 12g | Carbs: 55.1g | Protein: 8.1g | Sugars: 7g

---

Air Fryer Spanakopita Bites

Prep time: 10 minutes | Cook time: 12 minutes | Serves 4

- 4 sheets phyllo dough
- Baby spinach leaves: 2 cups
- Grated Parmesan cheese: 2 tablespoons
- Low-fat cottage cheese: 1/4 cup
- Dried oregano: 1 teaspoon
- Feta cheese: 6 tbsp. crumbled
- Water: 2 tablespoons
- One egg white only
- Lemon zest: 1 teaspoon
- Cayenne pepper: 1/8 teaspoon
- Olive oil: 1 tablespoon
- Kosher salt and freshly ground black pepper: 1/4 teaspoon, each

1. In a pot over high heat, add water and spinach, cook until wilted.
2. Drain it and cool for ten minutes. Squeeze out excess moisture.
3. In a bowl, mix Parmesan cheese, cottage cheese, egg white, cayenne pepper, spinach, oregano, salt, black pepper, feta cheese, and zest. Mix it well.
4. Lay one phyllo sheet on a flat surface. Spray with oil. Add the second sheet of phyllo on top—spray oil. Add a total of 4 oiled sheets.
5. Spray the air fryer basket with oil. Put eight bites in the basket and cook for 12 minutes at 375°F until golden brown. Flip halfway through.

PER SERVING

Calories: 81.7 | Fat: 3.8g | Protein: 3.6g | Carbs: 6.7g

Tomato Basil Soup

Prep time: 10 minutes | Cook time:25 minutes | Serves 4

- 4 Garlic cloves peeled
- 1/2 Cups chicken broth
- 1/2 Cup heavy cream
- 1/2 tsp. Oil
- 1 Lb. red tomatoes cut in half
- 1 Red bell pepper quartered
- 1 Yellow onion quartered
- 1 Carrot chopped
- 4 Fresh basil leaves chopped
- Splash of balsamic vinegar

1. Preheat the Air Fryer to 4000F. Pour some oil on the Air Fryer cooking basket. Put the tomatoes, red bell pepper, onion, carrot, garlic cloves to the Air Fryer.
2. Cook at 3600F for about 25 minutes. Shaking halfway through for proper cooking. Flip the vegetables onto a medium pan and place chicken broth.
3. Bring the mixture to a boil. Simmer for at least 5 minutes. Add the soup to an immersion blender and blend properly.
4. Put basil, heavy cream, balsamic vinegar, Salt, and pepper. Top with parmesan cheese.
5. Serve and enjoy!!!

PER SERVING

Calories:150 | Fat:10g |Carbohydrates: 14g | Protein: 2g

Chili Fingerling Potatoes

Prep time: 10 minutes | Cook time:16 minutes |Serves 4

- 1pound fingerling potatoes, rinsed and cut into wedges
- 1 teaspoon olive oil
- 1 teaspoon salt
- 1 teaspoon black pepper
- 1 teaspoon cayenne pepper
- 1 teaspoon Nutritional yeast
- 1/2 teaspoon garlic powder

1. Preheat the air fryer oven to 400F (204C).
2. Coat the potatoes with the rest of the ingredients. Transfer to the air fryer basket.
3. Place in the air fryer basket set time to 16 minutes, shaking the basket halfway through the cooking time.
4. Serve immediately.

PER SERVING

Calories:120 | Fat:4g |Carbohydrates: 20g | Protein: 2.4g

Air Fryer Avocado Fries

Prep time: 10 minutes | Cook time: 10 minutes | Serves 2

- One avocado
- One egg
- Whole wheat bread crumbs: 1/2 cup
- Salt: 1/2 teaspoon

1. Cut the avocado into wedges.
2. In a bowl, beat egg with salt. In another bowl, add the bread crumbs.
3. Coat wedges in egg, then in crumbs.
4. Air fry them at 400°F for 8-10 minutes. Toss halfway through.

PER SERVING

Calories: 250.5 | Carbs: 18.7g | Protein: 6.5g | Fat: 16.5g

Asparagus Avocado Soup

Prep time: 10 minutes | Cook time: 15 minutes | Serves 4

- 1 avocado, peeled, pitted, cubed
- 12 oz. asparagus
- 1/2 tsp. ground black pepper
- 1 tsp. garlic powder
- 1 tsp. sea salt
- 2 tbsp. olive oil, divided
- 1/2 lemon, juiced
- 2 cups vegetable stock

1. Set the fryer to 425°F, and preheat for 5 minutes.
2. Meanwhile, place the asparagus in a shallow dish, sprinkle with 1 tbsp. of oil, garlic powder, salt, and black pepper, and toss until mixed.
3. Open the fryer, add the asparagus, and cook for 10 minutes until roasted, shaking halfway through the frying.

4. Transfer asparagus to a food processor. Add the remaining ingredients into a food processor and pulse until well combined and smooth.
5. Tip the soup in a saucepan, pour in the water if it is too thick, and heat it over medium-low heat for 5 minutes until thoroughly heated. Ladle the soup into bowls and serve.

PER SERVING

Calories: 207.8 | Carbs: 12.8g | Fat: 15.4g | Protein: 6.3g | Fiber: 5g

Sweet Potato Cauliflower Patties

Prep time: 20 minutes | Cook time: 20 minutes | Serves 7

- 1 green onion, chopped
- 1 large sweet potato, peeled
- 1 tsp. garlic, minced
- 1 cup cilantro leaves
- 2 cup cauliflower florets
- 1/4 tsp. ground black pepper
- 1/4 tsp. salt
- 1/4 cup sunflower seeds
- 1/4 tsp. cumin
- 1/4 cup ground flaxseed
- 1/2 tsp. red chili powder
- 2 tbsp. ranch seasoning mix
- 2 tbsp. arrowroot starch

1. Cut peeled sweet potato into small pieces, then place them in a food processor and pulse until pieces are broken up.
2. Then add the garlic, cauliflower florets, onion, and pulse; add the remaining ingredients and pulse more until well combined.
3. Tip the mixture into a bowl, shape it into 7 1 1/2-inch thick patties, each about 1/4 cup, then place them on a baking sheet and freeze for 10 minutes.
4. Switch on the air fryer, insert the fryer basket, and grease it with olive oil; close the lid, set the fryer at 400°F, and preheat for 10 minutes.
5. Open the fryer, add patties to it in a single layer, and cook for 20 minutes; flipping the patties halfway through the frying.
6. When the air fryer beeps, open the lid, transfer the patties onto a serving plate, and keep them warm.
7. Prepare the continuing patties in the same way and serve.

PER SERVING

Calories: 84.5 | Carbs: 8.7g | Fat: 2.8g | Protein: 3.2g | Fiber: 3.5g

Chapter 9
Desserts

Raspberry Cookies In Air Fryer

Prep time: 15 minutes | Cook time: 7 minutes | Serves 10

- One teaspoon of baking powder
- One cup of almond flour
- Three tablespoons of natural low-calorie sweetener
- One large egg
- Four tablespoons of softened cream cheese

1. In a large bowl, add egg, flour, sweetener, baking powder, and cream cheese, mix well until a dough wet forms. Chill the dough in the fridge for 20 minutes.
2. Let the air fryer preheat to 400°F, add the parchment paper to the air fryer basket.
3. Make ten balls from the dough and put them in the prepared air fryer basket.
4. with your clean hands, make an indentation from your thumb in the center of every cookie. Add one teaspoon of the raspberry preserve in the thumb hole.
5. Bake in the air fryer for seven minutes.
6. Let the cookies cool completely in the parchment paper for almost 15 minutes.

PER SERVING

Calories: 110.2 | Protein: 3.8g | Carbs: 8.3g | Fat: 8.8g

Banana Muffins In Air Fryer

Prep time: 10 minutes | Cook time: 30 minutes | Serves 8

WET MIX:

- 3 tbsp. of milk
- Four Cavendish size, ripe bananas
- Half cup sugar alternative
- Two large eggs

DRY MIX:

- One teaspoon of baking powder
- One and a 1/4 cup of whole wheat flour
- One teaspoon of baking soda
- One teaspoon of cinnamon
- 2 tbsp. of cocoa powder
- One teaspoon of salt

1. with the fork, in a bowl, mash up the bananas, add all the wet ingredients to it, and mix well.
2. Sift all the dry ingredients so they combine well. Add into the wet ingredients. Carefully fold both ingredients together. Then add in the chopped walnuts, and slices of dried up fruits.
3. Let the air fryer preheat to 260°F.
4. Spray muffin cups with oil, and add the batter into. Air fryer for at least half an hour.
5. Take out from the air fryer and let them cool down before serving.

PER SERVING

Calories: 210.8 | Protein: 12.5g | Carbs: 17.5g | Fat: 11.5g

Carrot Cake with Vanilla Glaze

Prep time: 10 minutes | Cook time:30 minutes |Serves 6

- 1 tbsp ground flaxseed
- 3 tbsp water
- ½ cup cake flour
- ¼ tsp baking soda
- pinch of kosher salt
- ½ tsp ground cinnamon
- ½ cup granulated sugar
- ¼ cup canola oil
- ½ tsp pure vanilla extract
- ¼ cup unsweetened applesauce
- ¾ cup grated carrots
- 2 tbsp raisins
- 2 tbsp chopped walnuts
- ⅓ cup powdered sugar
- ½ tsp pure vanilla extract
- 2 tsp dairy-free milk (soy recommended)

1. Set the air fryer temp to 310°F. Spray a bundt pan with nonstick cooking spray. Set aside.
2. In a small bowl, combine the flaxseed and water. Set aside for at least 5 minutes.
3. In a large bowl, whisk together the cake flour, baking soda, salt, and cinnamon. Add the sugar, canola oil, vanilla extract, applesauce, and flaxseed mixture. Mix well. Fold in the carrots, raisins, and walnuts. Place the batter in the pan.
4. Place the pan in the fryer basket and bake until a toothpick comes out clean from the center, about 25 to 30 minutes. Turn off the air fryer and allow the pan to sit in the air fryer for 5 minutes.
5. Transfer the cake to a serving platter and allow to cool completely.
6. In a small bowl, make the glaze by whisking together the ingredients. Drizzle the glaze over the cake and allow to set.
7. Cut the cake into 6 slices before serving.

PER SERVING

Calories: 249 | Fat: 11g | Sat Fat: 1g | Cholesterol:0mg | Sodium: 85mg | Carbohydrates 37g | Fiber:1g | Sugar:27g | Protein:2g

Shortbread

Prep time: 10 minutes | Cook time: 8 minutes | Serves 6

- 250g self raising flour
- 175g butter
- 75g sugar

1. First, make a soft shortbread dough by rubbing butter into flour and sugar until it resembles breadcrumbs. If you haven't done so already, use a knife to chop the butter into tiny bits. Then rub the fat into the flour and sugar using your hands. Rub until it resembles breadcrumbs.
2. Then combine them together with your fingers until they form a soft dough.
3. Flour a clean kitchen worktop and flour a rolling pin too; then roll out your shortbread dough to about 0.5cm thick. Then cut out shapes depending on their desired size.
4. Then add a layer of foil into the air fryer basket and then place the shortbread over it.
5. Finally, air fry for almost 8 minutes at 180°C/360°F, then allow it to cool completely before storing in an airtight container.

PER SERVING

Calories: 408 | Fat: 24g | Carbs: 43g | Protein: 5g | Sugar: 13g | Sodium: 209mg

Lemon Zucchini Bread

Prep time:10 minutes |Cook time: 40 minutes |Serves 12

- 2 cups almond flour
- 2 teaspoons baking powder
- ¾ cup swerve
- ½ cup coconut oil, melted
- 1 teaspoon lemon juice
- 1 teaspoon vanilla extract
- 3 eggs, whisked
- 1 cup zucchini, shredded
- 1 tablespoon lemon zest Cooking spray

1. In a bowl, mix all the ingredients except the cooking spray and stir well.
2. Grease a loaf pan that fits the air fryer with the cooking spray, line with parchment paper and pour the loaf mix inside.
3. Put the pan in the air fryer and cook at 330 degrees F for 40 minutes.
4. Cool down, slice and serve.

PER SERVING

Calories 143| Fat 11| Fiber 1| Carbs 3| Protein 3

Orange Muffins

Prep time:10 minutes |Cook time: 10 minutes |Serves 5

- 5 eggs, beaten
- 1 tablespoon poppy seeds
- 1 teaspoon vanilla extract
- ¼ teaspoon ground nutmeg
- ½ teaspoon baking powder
- 1 teaspoon orange juice
- 1 teaspoon orange zest, grated
- 5 tablespoons coconut flour
- 1 tablespoon Monk fruit
- 2 tablespoons coconut flakes
- Cooking spray

1. In the mixing bowl mix up eggs, poppy seeds, vanilla extract, ground nutmeg, baking powder, orange juice, orange zest, coconut flour, and Monk fruit.
2. Add coconut flakes and mix up the mixture until it is homogenous and without any clumps.
3. Preheat the air fryer to 360F.
4. Spray the muffin molds with cooking spray from inside.
5. Pour the muffin batter in the molds and transfer them in the air fryer.
6. Cook the muffins for 10 minutes.

PER SERVING

calories 119| fat 7.1| fiber 3.4| carbs 6.2| protein 7.5

French Toast Bites

Prep time: 5 minutes | Cook time:15 minutes |Serves 8

- Almond milk
- Cinnamon
- Sweetener
- 3 eggs
- 4 pieces wheat bread

1. Preheat air fryer to 360 degrees F.
2. Whisk eggs and thin out with almond milk.
3. Mix 1/3 cup of sweetener with lots of cinnamon.
4. Tear bread in half, ball up pieces and press together to form a ball.
5. Soak bread balls in egg and then roll into cinnamon sugar, making sure to coat thoroughly.
6. Place coated bread balls into air fryer and bake 15 minutes.

PER SERVING

Calories:289 | Fat:11g |Carbohydrates: 45g | Protein: 5g

Crustless Cheesecake

Prep time: 5 minutes | Cook time: 10 minutes | Serves 2

- 16 oz. cream cheese, reduced-fat, softened
- 2 tbsp. sour cream, reduced-fat
- ¾ cup erythritol sweetener
- 1 tsp. vanilla extract, unsweetened
- 2 eggs, pastured
- ½ tsp. lemon juice

1. Set the air fryer at 350°F, and preheat for 5 minutes.
2. Take two 4 inches of springform pans, grease them with oil, and set them aside.
3. Crack the eggs in a bowl and then whisk in erythritol, lemon juice, and vanilla until smooth.
4. Whisk in cream cheese and sour cream until blended and then divide the mixture evenly between prepared pans.
5. Place springform pans in the air fryer and cook for 10 minutes.
6. Take out the cakes, and refrigerate for 3 hours before serving.

PER SERVING

Calories: 317.9 | Carbs: 0.9g | Fat: 29.1g | Protein: 12.1g | Fiber: 0g

Buttery Muffins

Prep time:15 minutes |Cook time: 10 minutes |Serves 2

- 1 teaspoon of cocoa powder
- 2 tablespoons coconut flour
- 2 teaspoons swerve
- ½ teaspoon vanilla extract
- 2 teaspoons almond butter, melted
- ¼ teaspoon baking powder
- 1 teaspoon apple cider vinegar
- ¼ teaspoon ground cinnamon

1. In the mixing bowl mix up cocoa powder, coconut flour, swerve, vanilla extract, almond butter, baking powder, and apple cider vinegar.
2. Then add ground cinnamon and stir the mixture with the help of the spoon until it is smooth.
3. Pour the brownie mixture in the muffin molds and leave for 10 minutes to rest.
4. Meanwhile, preheat the air fryer to 365F.
5. Put the muffins in the air fryer basket and cook them for 10 minutes.
6. Then remove the cooked brownie muffins from the air fryer and cool them completely.

PER SERVING

Calories 145| Fat 10.4| Fiber 5| Carbs 10.7| Protein 5.1

Cinnamon Sugar Roasted Chickpeas

Prep time: 10 minutes | Cook time:10 minutes |Serves 2

- 1 tbsp. sweetener
- 1 tbsp. cinnamon
- 1 C. chickpeas

1. Preheat the air fryer to 390 degrees F.
2. Rinse and drain chickpeas.
3. Mix all ingredients and add to the air fryer.
4. Cook 10 minutes.

PER SERVING

Calories:111 | Fat:4g |Carbohydrates: 16g | Protein: 4g

Apple Pies

Prep time: 10 minutes | Cook time:10 minutes |Serves 1

- 1 medium apple (Gala or Granny Smith recommended), peeled and finely diced
- juice of ½ orange
- 2 tbsp granulated sugar
- ½ tsp ground cinnamon
- 2 tsp cornstarch
- 10oz (285g) vegan pie dough
- all-purpose flour

1. Set the air fryer temp to 350°F.
2. In a large bowl, combine the apple, orange juice, sugar, cinnamon, and cornstarch. Mix well.
3. Roll out the dough on a lightly floured surface. Cut the dough into 4 rounds. Place 2 tablespoons of the apple mixture in the center of each. Fold the dough in half and seal the edges with a fork. Make a small slit in the top for steam to escape.
4. Place the pies in the fryer basket and cook until golden brown, about 10 minutes. Turn off the air fryer and allow the pies to cool in the fryer basket for 2 to 3 minutes.
1. Transfer the pies to a wire rack to cool before serving.

PER SERVING

Calories: 220 | Fat: 10g | Sat Fat: 1g | Cholesterol:0mg | Sodium: 205mg | Carbohydrates 31g | Fiber:2g | Sugar:13g | Protein:2g

Nut Bars

Prep time:15 minutes |Cook time: 30 minutes |Serves 10

- ½ cup coconut oil, softened
- 1 teaspoon baking powder
- 1 teaspoon lemon juice
- 1 cup almond flour
- ½ cup coconut flour
- 3 tablespoons Erythritol
- 1 teaspoon vanilla extract
- 2 eggs, beaten
- 2 oz hazelnuts, chopped
- 1 oz macadamia nuts, chopped
- Cooking spray

1. In the mixing bowl mix up coconut oil and baking powder.
2. Add lemon juice, almond flour, coconut flour, Erythritol, vanilla extract, and eggs.
3. Stir the mixture until it is smooth or use the immersion blender for this step.
4. Then add hazelnuts and macadamia nuts.
5. Stir the mixture until homogenous.
6. After this, preheat the air fryer to 325F.
7. Line the air fryer basket with baking paper.
8. Then pour the nut mixture in the air fryer basket and flatten it well with the help of the spatula.
9. Cook the mixture for 30 minutes.
10. Then cool the mixture well and cut it into the serving bars.

PER SERVING

Calories 208| Fat 19.8| Fiber 3.5| Carbs 9.5| Protein 4

Baked Apple
Prep time: 10 minutes | Cook time:10 minutes |Serves 4

- 1/4 C. water
- 1/4 tsp. nutmeg
- 1/4 tsp. cinnamon
- 1 1/2 tsp. melted ghee
- 2 tbsp. raisins
- 2 tbsp. chopped walnuts
- 1 medium apple

1. Preheat your air fryer to 350 degrees.
2. Slice an apple in half and discard some of the flesh from the center.
3. Place into a frying pan.
4. Mix remaining ingredients together except water. Spoon mixture to the middle of apple halves.
5. Pour water overfilled apples.
6. Place pan with apple halves into the air fryer, bake 20 minutes.

PER SERVING

Calories:199 | Fat:9g |Carbohydrates: 17g | Protein: 1g

Air Fryer Blueberry Muffins
Prep time: 10 minutes | Cook time: 12 minutes | Serves 8

- Half cup of sugar alternative
- One and 1/3 cup of flour
- 1/3 cup of oil
- Two teaspoons of baking powder
- 1/4 teaspoon of salt
- One egg
- Half cup of milk
- 2/3 cup of frozen and thawed blueberries, or fresh

1. Let the air fryer preheat to 330 F.
2. In a large bowl, sift together sugar alternative, baking powder, salt, and flour. Mix well.
3. In another bowl, add milk, oil, and egg. Mix it well.
4. Combine the dry ingredients to the egg mixture, and mix. Add the blueberries and pour the mixture into muffin paper cups.
5. Cook muffins for 12-14 minutes and let them cool before serving.

PER SERVING

Calories: 210.5 | Protein: 9.2g | Carbs: 12.8g | Fat: 9.8g

Stuffed Apples

Prep time: 10 minutes | Cook time:20 minutes |Serves 4

- 2 small red or green apples, halved horizontally
- 4 tsp vegan butter (Earth Balance recommended)
- ¼ tsp ground cardamom
- 2 tsp ground cinnamon
- ¼ cup chopped walnuts
- ¼ cup raisins
- pinch of kosher salt

1. Set the air fryer temp to 350°F.
2. Remove the seeds and core from both halves of each apple and place all 4 halves cut side up in a baking dish. Pour about 1 inch (2.5cm) of water into the bottom of the dish.
3. In a medium bowl, combine the butter, cardamom, cinnamon, walnuts, raisins, and salt. Mix well. Equally divide the filling among the apple halves.
4. Place the dish in the fryer basket and bake until the apples are tender, about 20 minutes.
5. Remove the dish from the fryer basket and allow the apples to cool for 10 minutes before serving.

PER SERVING

Calories: 135 | Fat: 6g | Sat Fat: 0g | Cholesterol:0mg | Sodium: 209mg | Carbohydrates 20g | Fiber:4g | Sugar:14g | Protein:2g

Lemon Butter Bars

Prep time:10 minutes |Cook time: 35 minutes |Serves 8

- ½ cup butter, melted
- 1 cup erythritol
- 1 and ¾ cups almond flour
- 3 eggs, whisked
- Zest of 1 lemon, grated
- Juice of 3 lemons

1. In a bowl, mix 1 cup flour with half of the erythritol and the butter, stir well and press into a baking dish that fits the air fryer lined with parchment paper.
2. Put the dish in your air fryer and cook at 350 degrees F for 10 minutes.
3. Meanwhile, in a bowl, mix the rest of the flour with the remaining erythritol and the other ingredients and whisk well.
4. Spread this over the crust, put the dish in the air fryer once more and cook at 350 degrees F for 25 minutes.
5. Cool down, cut into bars and serve.

PER SERVING

Calories 210| Fat 12| Fiber 1| Carbs 4| Protein 8

Chocolate Lava Cake

Prep time: 5 minutes | Cook time: 13 minutes | Serves 2

- 1 tbsp. flax meal
- ½ tsp. baking powder
- 1 tbsp. cocoa powder, unsweetened
- ½ tbsp. erythritol sweetener
- ⅛ tsp. Stevia sweetener
- ⅛ tsp. vanilla extract, unsweetened
- 1 tbsp. olive oil
- 2 tbsp. water
- 1 egg, pastured

1. Set the air fryer at 350°F, and preheat for 5 minutes.
2. Meanwhile, take two cups of the ramekin, grease it with oil, and set it aside.
3. Place all the ingredients in a bowl, whisk until incorporated, and pour the batter into the ramekin.
4. Open the fryer, place ramekin in it, close with its lid, and cook for 8 minutes until inserting a skewer into the cake slides out clean.
5. Let the cake cool before cutting into slices, and serve.

PER SERVING

Calories: 362.1 | Carbs: 3.2g | Fat: 32.9g | Protein: 12.1g | Fiber: 0.6g

Thai Fried Bananas

Prep time: 20 minutes | Cook time: 40 minutes | Serves 4

- 4 ripe bananas
- 2 tablespoons rice flour
- 2 tablespoons desiccated coconut
- 1/2 teaspoon baking powder
- oil , to drizzle
- sesame seeds
- 1/4 cup rice flour
- 1/2 teaspoon cardamom powder
- 1 pinch salt
- 2 tablespoons corn flour
- 2 tablespoons all-purpose flour

1. To make fried bananas, gather the ingredients together and keep them handy. We'll begin by making the batter for the fried bananas.
2. Add all-purpose flour, rice flour, corn flour, baking powder, salt, and coconut into a large bowl, and stir to combine well. Add a little amount of water at a time until you get a thick and almost smooth batter.
3. Coat the banana slices in batter and roll them in rice flour and sesame seeds.
4. Then place them in a greased foil or butter paper for air frying at 200°C for almost 10 – 15 minutes until golden browned. Serve with ice cream for dessert.

PER SERVING

Calories: 191| Fat: 5.7g | Carbs: 37g | Protein: 1.59g | Sugar: 20g | Sodium: 12.1mg

Appendix 1 Measurement Conversion Chart

Volume Equivalents (Dry)

US STANDARD	METRIC (APPROXIMATE)
1/8 teaspoon	0.5 mL
1/4 teaspoon	1 mL
1/2 teaspoon	2 mL
3/4 teaspoon	4 mL
1 teaspoon	5 mL
1 tablespoon	15 mL
1/4 cup	59 mL
1/2 cup	118 mL
3/4 cup	177 mL
1 cup	235 mL
2 cups	475 mL
3 cups	700 mL
4 cups	1 L

Volume Equivalents (Liquid)

US STANDARD	US STANDARD (OUNCES)	METRIC (APPROXIMATE)
2 tablespoons	1 fl.oz.	30 mL
1/4 cup	2 fl.oz.	60 mL
1/2 cup	4 fl.oz.	120 mL
1 cup	8 fl.oz.	240 mL
1 1/2 cup	12 fl.oz.	355 mL
2 cups or 1 pint	16 fl.oz.	475 mL
4 cups or 1 quart	32 fl.oz.	1 L
1 gallon	128 fl.oz.	4 L

Temperatures Equivalents

FAHRENHEIT(F)	CELSIUS(C) APPROXIMATE)
225 °F	107 °C
250 °F	120 ° °C
275 °F	135 °C
300 °F	150 °C
325 °F	160 °C
350 °F	180 °C
375 °F	190 °C
400 °F	205 °C
425 °F	220 °C
450 °F	235 °C
475 °F	245 °C
500 °F	260 °C

Weight Equivalents

US STANDARD	METRIC (APPROXIMATE)
1 ounce	28 g
2 ounces	57 g
5 ounces	142 g
10 ounces	284 g
15 ounces	425 g
16 ounces (1 pound)	455 g
1.5 pounds	680 g
2 pounds	907 g

Appendix 2 The Dirty Dozen and Clean Fifteen

The Environmental Working Group (EWG) is a nonprofit, nonpartisan organization dedicated to protecting human health and the environment Its mission is to empower people to live healthier lives in a healthier environment. This organization publishes an annual list of the twelve kinds of produce, in sequence, that have the highest amount of pesticide residue-the Dirty Dozen-as well as a list of the fifteen kinds ofproduce that have the least amount of pesticide residue-the Clean Fifteen.

THE DIRTY DOZEN	
The 2016 Dirty Dozen includes the following produce. These are considered among the year's most important produce to buy organic:	
Strawberries	Spinach
Apples	Tomatoes
Nectarines	Bell peppers
Peaches	Cherry tomatoes
Celery	Cucumbers
Grapes	Kale/collard greens
Cherries	Hot peppers

The Dirty Dozen list contains two additional itemskale/collard greens and hot peppers-because they tend to contain trace levels of highly hazardous pesticides.

THE CLEAN FIFTEEN	
The least critical to buy organically are the Clean Fifteen list. The following are on the 2016 list:	
Avocados	Papayas
Corn	Kiw
Pineapples	Eggplant
Cabbage	Honeydew
Sweet peas	Grapefruit
Onions	Cantaloupe
Asparagus	Cauliflower
Mangos	

Some of the sweet corn sold in the United States are made from genetically engineered (GE) seedstock. Buy organic varieties of these crops to avoid GE produce.

Appendix 3 Index

NADIA K. THEISEN

Printed in Great Britain
by Amazon